Adventures High Seas on the

"A travel journal with unexpected encounters"

Joyce D. Giguere

WESTBOW
PRESS®
A DIVISION OF THOMAS NELSON
& ZONDERVAN

WestBow Press books may be ordered through booksellers or by contacting:

WestBow Press
A Division of Thomas Nelson & Zondervan
1663 Liberty Drive
Bloomington, IN 47403
www.westbowpress.com
844-714-3454

ISBN: 978-1-6642-2321-9 (sc)
ISBN: 978-1-6642-2322-6 (hc)
ISBN: 978-1-6642-2323-3 (e)

Library of Congress Control Number: 2021902710

Print information available on the last page.

WestBow Press rev. date: 04/15/2021

Dedicated

To my husband, Jack, whose patience and love
sustains me.

and

Jack and Alex
Our grandsons,
for whom these journals were written
so they would know what Grandma and "Ole Gramps"
are up to in their retirement years.

Acknowledgements

One never arrives at this junction without having to thank so many for their encouragement, invaluable help and wonderful ideas.

I must thank Jack, my husband, for getting me into this project and holding my hand the whole way. For Andrew our placement agent then for Holland America Line, for giving Jack the opportunity to serve in ministry in this incredible way, Haines and Nancy Holt who, for five years, drove us to the airport hotel making sure we arrived at our plane on time and were there at the conclusion four months later to drive us back home again. Also to Bob and Jacquie Paul, who generously gave us their friendship and included us on many of their tours that we would not have had the opportunity to enjoy otherwise. For Ernie and Bert Fickerson, travel guides who became friends on ship, and who personally taught us how to navigate with courage and confidence around the world on our own in many exotic ports. For my journal group who received these journals weekly and expressed delight in traveling with us through the written word.

Publishing is never in a vacuum and the agents and staff at Westbow Press have been a highly dedicated group of people who have guided me every step of the way. I cannot begin to thank them enough. Mostly, Jack and I both thank Holland America Line for the opportunity to minister on the high seas around the world for five years. They are one of the very few cruise lines that carry a protestant chaplain, priest and rabbi on extended cruises. We are grateful for their commitment to the spiritual and emotional needs of their passengers.

Introduction

Adventures on the High Seas

For five years I had the rare privilege of being selected as the Protestant chaplain for five Holland America Line's Grand World Cruises. This book is the story of our first such cruise, just as it happened.

My wife Joyce and I both retired in 1999, she as a clinical dietitian for St. John Hospital in Detroit and myself from the pastorate at Grosse Pointe United Methodist Church, Grosse Pointe, Michigan. Because we had always wanted to travel, it wasn't long before we began taking trips on cruise ships. First to the Caribbean, then Alaska and the Maritime Provinces of Canada, and down to the Panama Canal. Almost always it was with Holland America Line. There were chaplains on these cruises, but I didn't think too much about it, having just retired and having no desire at that time to return to pastoral duties.

However, our Panama cruise came not long after Joyce's last hip replacement surgery, and when Sunday came around, she said she was going to rest in bed and not attend the onboard worship service. I, however, went, and when I returned to the stateroom, she asked, "Why don't you look into being a cruise ship chaplain? It might save us tons of money."

So I went to the front desk and asked, "Under whose direction do the chaplains work on the ship?"

"The Entertainment Department," came the reply; "the

chaplains work under the Cruise Director." That surprised me, so I asked if that was true as well at the corporate office for Holland America in Seattle, Washington. "Yes," she replied, "it comes under the Entertainment Department there too." When we got home I sent a letter off, addressing it to Holland America Line and attention of the Entertainment Department. It was one page telling about myself and saying I was interested in their chaplain program.

One week later I received a call from Holland America. The caller identified himself and said, "I have your letter in my hand and we are very interested in you. Are you immediately available?"

I replied, "I'm available, but what do you mean by immediately?"

He said, "We have openings in the next two months." He then said, "The agent who handles our chaplains is in New York City. I'll call him now and tell him about you, and I want you to call him first thing in the morning. He'll email all the forms you will need to fill out, and then we will put you to work."

I then asked, "Can you give me some basic information of what will be required of me?"

He said, "For the cruises to which you will be assigned there will be a daily fee of thirty dollars. which you will pay the agent. You will care for your own transportation costs to and from the ship, your visas, insurance, and medical shots if needed, and for the ship tours you might like to take. Those will be your only costs." Then he added, "By the way, I notice you are a graduate of Albion College"—a United Methodist college in Michigan—"and your last church was in Grosse Pointe, Michigan."

"Yes," I said proudly.

Then he added, "I am a graduate of Adrian College"—another United Methodist college in Michigan—"and I am familiar with Grosse Pointe." I said to myself, *I wonder if that is the reason my letter rose to the top on his desk.*

I followed his instructions, and the first cruise to which we were assigned was a fifteen-day Hawaiian Island cruise out of San

Diego, California. We were housed in a staff cabin, and I provided a daily morning prayer service and Sunday services and made myself available for spiritual needs of the passengers as they arose. Before we left on that cruise, I received a second assignment. It was a two-week Mediterranean cruise out of Rome. Using frequent flier miles with British Air, we booked our flights and made hotel reservations in London for a few days on our return. All those arrangements were made before we left on our first assignment to Hawaii.

While on the Hawaiian cruise, I noted that Holland America had several sixty-day cruises. One was to Australia and Asia, one to Africa and the Mediterranean, and another to South America. I told Joyce, "I'd like to learn about one of those for next year." So, when we got home I called the agent in New York and asked about them.

He told me, "Those cruises are by invitation only. Chaplains on those cruises have to do more than conduct services. They are required to teach each day the ship is at sea. If you'd like to be considered and have teaching experience, send me a list of what you can teach." I responded by sending him a list of what I had taught regarding the ancient world of Greece, Rome, Egypt, and the Holy Land and gave it the general title "Windows on the Biblical World."

One week later the agent called to say, "The chaplain for the 2008 Grand World Cruise is ill. I'm calling to invite you to replace him." I knew nothing about Holland America's World Cruise and asked him to tell me about it. He said, "It is a cruise which literally circles the globe, taking four months, and Holland America takes three chaplains, a Roman Catholic priest, a Jewish rabbi, and a Protestant pastor." At that point I sat down. "Unlike the other Holland America cruises," he continued, "the daily fee is waived. You will have a regular passenger stateroom, not a staff cabin, and Holland America will cover all other costs. They will provide laundry service, give you the crew discounts on internet use and a phone card, as well as any purchases you make on the ship. In addition, they will make and pay for all your travel arrangements to and from the ship." I could not believe what I was hearing.

He continued, "You will conduct services for the passengers, of which there will be about 1,200, and services for the Christians among the 700-member crew. You will conduct prayer and memorial services when requested, and you will teach each day the ship is at sea, which is between fifty-four and sixty days. There are just three prohibitions. You and your wife must never be intoxicated, you are never to be seen in the casino, and you are never to take the front row seats at the live evening entertainment shows."

Under my breath I said to myself, "No problem." Then, thinking about the flight reservations we had made for Rome, I asked, "What about the Mediterranean cruise you assigned me to?" He said he would find a replacement. And then, realizing Joyce was not home, I said, "I need to speak to my wife, and she is not here at the moment."

He replied, "I need your answer in twenty-four hours."

When Joyce got home, I took the packages from her hands and asked her to sit down. Looking at me with a concerned expression, she asked, "Who died?"

I responded, "No one has died. Santa Claus has come early." I then told her everything the agent had shared with me. Her response? "We can't do that. We always meet the children and grandchildren in Florida during the winter."

Trying to convince her otherwise, I said, "Joyce, this is a once-in-a-lifetime opportunity that may never come again. I'd really like to accept the offer." Together we decided that this was an unusual opportunity, and within the hour I called my agent back and accepted the assignment. We had three and half weeks to get our visas, medical shots, and insurance arranged as well as put my class and sermon notes together. And during that time, we traveled to Vermont for Christmas with our family. When we got home, we had three days to pack and get ready.

Our first Grand World Cruise in 2008 was a fantastic experience. It was Holland American's 50th anniversary cruise on their flagship MS *Amsterdam*, and they pulled out all the stops to make it perfect. It was a circumnavigation of the world following the sun on its westward journey. We visited thirty-nine ports in twenty-seven countries on five continents, transiting both the Panama and Suez Canals. And when we returned to New York City, fireboats with their sprays greeted us, and as we sailed past the Statue of Liberty a plane circled the ship carrying a banner which read: 'Welcome Home MS *Amsterdam*."

During the last month of that trip, passengers asked, "Have they invited you back for next year?" I reminded them that I was a substitute for the pastor who was ill, and I was sure that once he recovered, he would be invited to return. And he was, but his doctor told him that his health was such that he could not do another world cruise. Consequently, a week after our return home my agent called to tell me Holland America wanted us back next year. In total they invited us back for five Grand World Cruises.

Each year we have met wonderful people from all over the world who take this world cruise. In the classes I taught were Jews, Roman Catholics, and Protestants of every variety as well as those without faith, some of whom also attended the secular humanists group that also met on the ship. My teaching confirms that people are drawn more by spiritual questions than by religious answers. Using the historical, literary, and cultural scholarship that has emerged over the last fifty years to revolutionize our view of the Bible, I have discovered that St. Augustine was correct when he said: "Just as there are shallows where a lamb may wade, so there are depths where an elephant may swim."

I learned again what every pastor experiences. That the ministry we provide reaches beyond the services conducted and the classes taught. It includes the quiet conversations in the halls, the intimate asides at social events as well as the prayers over phone lines between staterooms. Just as in the church, on the ship I've seen despair lifted, guilt relieved, hope restored, human will pushed to new resolve, and minds enlivened with the imponderables of our faith.

That is why when we packed for each World Cruise sailing, I could say with Jessie Adams:

> I feel the winds of God today; today my sail I lift,
> Though heavy, oft with drenching spray, and torn with many a rift;
> If hope but light the water's crest, and Christ my bark will use,
> I'll seek the seas at his behest, and brave another cruise.

The Rev. Dr. Jack E. Giguere

Grand World Cruise - 2008
Golden Anniversary of Holland America World Cruises
Sailed Friday, January 4, 2008
MS *Amsterdam* with
Captain Edward G. vanZaane

A very wise person once said, "Travel is the only thing you can buy that will make you richer." If, indeed, this is true, Jack and I will be very wealthy people. God has blessed us tremendously.

Joyce D. Giguere
January 4, 2008

JOURNAL # 1

Friday, January 4

Our day began early, at 3:00 a.m., in Easton, Maryland. At 4:30 a.m., Nancy and Haines Holt graciously took us to BWI Airport for our flight to the ship docked at Fort Lauderdale, Florida. We arrived at the ship at 12:30 p.m. and were admitted through the staffing entrance and directly on board. It was the quickest and easiest boarding we have ever experienced.

Our first day was taken with all the business necessary for Jack as the ship's resident Protestant chaplain. We met the cruise director, who is Jack's immediate supervisor, at an introductory meeting in the Queen's Lounge. We also became acquainted with Father Bill, the Catholic priest, and Bob and Sheila Gan, the Jewish rabbi and his wife. They are all friendly and lovely people, and we look forward to getting better acquainted. We met many of the other staff members as well.

Our room is a regular guest cabin and not the usual staff cabin. It is lovely and has a window. A real treat. It is serviced several times a day, including even chocolates on our pillows at night. We had our meals at the Lido cafeteria today due to a busy schedule and made arrangements with the hotel dining manager to be "floaters" at dinner. They scheduled us at 8:30 p.m., and with Jack's hypoglycemia, we cannot eat that late. So we will go to the dining room at 6:00 p.m., and they will seat us where there is an empty place. We have met great people this way and were amazed to learn that for some people, this is their sixth world cruise.

Jack was to be at the introductory show to welcome those aboard and to be introduced with the other staff members. This was at 8:00 p.m. and 10:15 p.m. After such a busy, early, and exhausting day, I passed and went straight to the shower and bed. Tomorrow will be a sea day on our way to the Grand Cayman Islands in the Caribbean Sea. We left the dock at 8:00 p.m.

Thank you, God, for a safe and easy journey to Fort Lauderdale. Our luggage arrived well with no overweights. This is a real feat.

Saturday, January 5

After a good, restful night of sleep on this gently rocking ship, we awoke to a bright, beautiful day in the Caribbean. Jack taught his first Bible class, "Windows on the Biblical World," at 9:00 a.m. and was pleased that twenty-some people came on the first day. He reported that they were an enthusiastic group and responded readily to discussion. We walked the decks for exercise and then filled out forms to be escorts for the shore excursions. That will involve assisting the guides, directing and shepherding the guests on tours, and then evaluating in detail each tour itself. For doing this, we receive the tours free of charge. Can't beat that.

I spent a frustrating few hours in the afternoon trying to get our laptop to work, only to find out we didn't have the proper wireless card. Oh well. Tomorrow is another day. We were able to get a staff discount internet access card for $20 for 200 minutes instead of the usual guest access for $100 for 250 minutes. Now if we can only get it to work.

The highlight of the day was meeting at lunch and dinner several couples who were a delight. We have met several people who will be on board for the full cruise around the globe. More than we imagined. After dinner, we went to the theater and saw

Regis Philbin, of *Live with Regis and Kelly* TV fame. He was wonderfully entertaining and is on board as a passenger. We look to tomorrow with joy as we dock at Grand Cayman and Jack has the first worship service in the Wajang Theatre.

Sunday, January 6 (Twelfth Day of Christmas)

Today was clear, sunny, and hot at 82.4 degrees Fahrenheit. We went on shore today at George Town, Cayman Islands, and strolled along the harbor with beautiful beaches and crystal-clear water. Most shops were closed on Sunday, and we were unable to go to the National Museum. It was under renovation because of severe damage from Hurricane Ivan. How very fragile these islands are to nature, and how brave these people are to live here.

We were tendered back to the ship at noon for lunch and met an interesting couple who knew Michigan, our summer residence, and Bay View well. The man had been raised in the upper peninsula of Michigan. It is wonderful that when we tell people that Jack is the chaplain on board, they immediately share about their churches and their faith journey. We also learned today that out of 1,300 guests on board, 1,100 are continuing completely around the world.

Jack's first worship service was at 5:00 p.m. today. It is in the evening on Sundays that we are in port, and 9:00 a.m. on Sundays we are at sea. The Wajang Theatre, where services were held, was quite full. More than a hundred attended and were very responsive.

After a delicious dinner where we dined alone tonight, we went to see a classical guitarist. The music and his skills were beautiful. His name is Carlos Bonell, and he is from London; he is currently composing a guitar concerto with Sir Paul McCartney of Beatles fame.

We set our clocks back one hour tonight and look forward to a restful sea day tomorrow.

Monday, January 7

Clear and hot today, temperature in the eighties. We awoke and had breakfast at 8:00 a.m. Jack's class went well and is growing. More than forty people attended. Discussion was very active, and people were not shy to question and give comments. I attended a presentation on the gemstone of emeralds by a noted gemologist, Mr. Chadwick, from London. Their history and legends are fascinating, and their rarity is amazing. I was amazed to learn that to have occlusions (flaws) is normal and proves that it is a natural emerald and not made in a laboratory.

We began our exercising in earnest today by walking the decks—Jack for one hour and I for one mile—and we are determined not to use the elevators. We also began our emailing for a trial on the staff computers, and it worked well. We will begin journaling and sending the entries soon to the journaling group I've created from email addresses.

It was a relaxing sea day today, and we're finally beginning to feel rested after all the preparations to get this far in our journey.

Formal night was tonight for dinner and theater. It was lovely, and everyone looked beautiful in gowns and tuxes. Of course, the food was wonderful. I can see that exercising will be necessary for both of us. The show was performed by the entertainment staff. They were quite good and talented young people. At the theater, I met a lovely lady from Severna Park, Maryland. The world is very small, even as we sail these vast, vast oceans.

Tomorrow we dock at the port of Limón, Costa Rica.

Tuesday, January 8

Awoke today to a cloudy, hot, and rainy morning of seventy-five degrees Fahrenheit. It cleared quickly to be hot and humid. After breakfast, we went ashore in Puerto Limón, Costa Rica. We did not plan an excursion as we had been here before but walked around the harbor, looked in the craft stalls from local craftsmen, took pictures of the port, and returned to the ship. We walked our mile and then investigated the exercise room, beginning our program for fitness. We had lunch with several couples and were able to encourage a lady who has diabetes and lost her monitor to ask for assistance from the cruise director. She promised she would do so. We had a restful afternoon, reading and computing. Jack was able to have copies made of a prayer he had read in his class by William Barclay for those of his class requesting it.

We shared dinner with an interesting couple from Louisiana. This is their fifth world cruise, and they have signed on for the next HAL world cruise in 2009. They are Roman Catholic and shared with us their strict childhood in the faith and expressed their thankfulness that attitudes have changed so drastically in their lifetime regarding acceptance of all faiths. We talked with them of our Catholic families and the acceptance we experienced in our lives as well. We continue to marvel that people are so open and almost hungry to speak of their faith journey. We saw a funny comedian this evening. Laughter is so good for the soul.

We will go through the Panama Canal tomorrow. There will be celebrations on deck all day as we progress through all the locks. This will begin at 6:30 a.m., and we will dock at Fuerte Amador, Panama, tomorrow around 8:00 p.m. Jack will teach his class again tomorrow. It is so good to be here.

Wednesday, January 9

Awoke today to a hot and overcast sky as we proceeded through the first set of Gatun Locks of the canal. It was thrilling to be at this historic site, and the lecturer narrated about the canal throughout the day. People spent most of the day on deck, watching the progress. At lunch, we made arrangements to meet a nice couple from Missouri, Lovet and Fred, and enjoyed conversation. We watched as we went through the second set of locks, called the Pedro Miguel Locks. At about 2:00 p.m., we went through the third set of locks, the Miraflores Locks. It took about one hour to go through each set. At the last set before the Pacific Ocean, at a huge building with many balconies, several hundred native people gathered, and they were chanting, singing, and cheering us on our journey through the canal. It was a lovely tradition on the Panamanian people's part, and we were touched.

Jack's class went very well, but fewer people attended because of the celebrations on deck all day. We did our daily exercises and then spent most of the afternoon on deck with everyone else. We had dinner at a table with three other couples. We enjoyed their company very much. We were concerned about one of the women because she is undergoing tests at Panama City tomorrow for suspicion that she may have appendicitis and may have to be airlifted back to the U.S. She is in our prayers this evening.

We do not have a tour tomorrow but will search for an Apple Store to purchase an Airport wireless card for our laptop. We are determined to get our computer problem resolved. Meanwhile, we have been using the crew internet room very successfully. We arrived at Amador, Panama, at about 4:30 p.m. today and will be tendered in to shore tomorrow.

Thursday, January 10, 2008

Today was a beautiful day in Amador, and we were looking forward to go ashore to search for the Apple Store in Panama City. The cruise shopping guide, Barbara, told us to go into the port building and speak with a guide there. The guide was a beautiful Panamanian lady who told us to go to the MultiPlaza and paged a taxi for us. The driver took us into Panama City, about twenty minutes from the dock. This was the most magnificent, upscale shopping mall we have ever seen, and there were three stories of fabulous stores. We very readily noticed driving in Panama City that there didn't appear to be a "middle" class of people. Others who toured the interior of Panama told us the same. A very, very poor class and obviously a very, very rich society.

At the Apple Store in the mall, the English speaking young man was unable to help us but directed us to the Mac tech support center and store in the city. We were fortunate to find a wonderful taxi driver who took us from the mall to the tech center. He came into the center to translate for us and waited for us to take us back to the mall. In a matter of a half hour our problems were solved. An airport wireless card was installed and reconfigured. What a joy! Our cab driver took us back to the mall so that we could continue walking and shopping. After noon, we tendered back to our ship. We set up our computer, and we're in business again and can pay bills and be in contact with friends and family.

After lunch, Jack was walking on deck when a man from Sweden approached him. Having been in Jack's classes, he felt free to tell Jack about his very wayward life. At his lowest time of complete despair and desperation, he asked God to change him. His life has never been the same. They continued to talk about his spiritual journey and how completely he has changed. We are continually blessed with people sharing their stories and lives with us. We have never experienced such openness.

We sat at the same table again tonight with three wonderful couples. They asked that we continue with them for the duration, and we agreed to do so. We hold hands and say grace before our meals, and we were so happy to learn that Jacquie, who we feared had appendicitis, does not have it but is now on stronger antibiotics for an infection. She is improving and will be remaining on ship with us. Praise God.

We set sail tonight at 6:00 p.m. for eight days at sea. Looking forward to the relaxation and friendships that are beginning to form.

Hello again, dear ones everywhere:

Here is our second installment of this amazing adventure. We are having a great time and enjoy meeting and getting acquainted with the other clergy on board. The people are wonderful, and we are making, I'm sure, lifelong friends. There is a certain bonding when you have crossed the equator together.

In addition, we are developing a very special relationship with those in Jack's class. When you know you will be together as closely as we are and probably never see each other beyond this world adventure, you cut right to the chase and begin a relationship that would take far longer at home. We speak of our faith journey quickly and readily to each other. Part of Jack's job is to engage the crew members in conversation, and it is no burden, believe me. Most are young men who are away from their families for many months at a time, who really are people who love to talk about their wives and children and also their parents and their homeland. Most are from Indonesia and the Philippines. Beautiful, caring people, and not just because they are paid to do so.

We pray all of you are well, and we love to hear from each of you. It's a strange feeling to be so far from home even when every need is met. Maybe, because if you are in the middle of the Pacific Ocean, thousands of miles from land, there is nowhere else you can go. God is very close.

Love and good wishes to each of you reading this.

Joyce and Jack

JOURNAL # 2

Today was a sea day, and we cannot believe that we have been cruising for one week. The time goes so quickly because there is so much to enjoy and so many people with which to visit. In seven days we will arrive at the port of Nuku Hiva in the French Polynesians, and tomorrow we will pass the Galapagos Islands about two hundred miles off our port side.

Jack's class is growing livelier as everyone gets better acquainted and less shy. We are sensing that some are a bit fearful of the actual history, and others soaking it up like sponges. Most have never been exposed to the history and culture of the first century and are quite amazed to learn how well educated Jesus was and that he could read. This was a rarity in the first century, and the disciples were probably illiterate. That too was usual in that time, and that caused a flurry of excitement and questions.

The beauty of sea days is that you can do as much or as little as your energy level allows. After exercising and lunch, rest is still attractive; so is reading. We had informal at dinner and theatre tonight. We all look so nice dressed up. At dinner all our tablemates were present, and one man bought a Panama hat in Panama City. We learned that Panama hats (the real ones) are made not in Panama but in Ecuador. During the building of the canal a hat maker in Ecuador was contracted to make special hats for the workers so they wouldn't get sunstroke. They also became very popular with the native people, and the Panama hat business boomed. The black hatband was added to mourn the death of Queen Victoria and has remained.

After dinner, we enjoyed a wonderful piano concert at the Queen's Lounge by a young Russian woman, Natativa Lavroan. We look forward to another beautiful day tomorrow.

Saturday, January 12

Today is cloudy with rainy showers throughout the day. Jack's class was fascinating, and the scripture was Mark 10:13 (NRSV), about bringing the children to Jesus and the disciples rebuking them. We learned of the status of the children; although loved, they ranked last in the family structure and had little value. One man in the class is a Roman Catholic and a student of Confucius; one lady born and raised in Cairo, Egypt, reads the Christian Bible in Hebrew and Aramaic. The class is growing daily and had more than fifty people today.

After our exercise, I attended a lecture by Gary Pudney, an executive producer from Hollywood who knew and told about the life of Elizabeth Taylor, the last *star* from the "Golden Age" of Hollywood. She is now seventy-five years old, has given up acting, is in a wheelchair, and devotes her life to her foundation for the awareness and cure of AIDS.

Today I began my project of knitting a baby afghan for my niece, Jenny, who is expecting a baby girl in April before we return to the US. With any luck, she will receive it before she is three years old.

The evening was formal tonight with a Black & White Dinner and Ball. The dining room and lounge were decorated beautifully with black and white fabric hangings, balloons, and beach balls. We wore only black and white formal wear. It was lovely and such fun. We saw Dick Hardwick, a very funny comedian who just returned from entertaining the troops in Iraq. We set our clocks back again tonight one hour. I love the ship's movement as it is so relaxing and calming. We sleep like two babies.

Sunday, January 13

It is a beautiful, hot, sunny, and windy day. Worship was well attended with over 150 present. There was standing room only. Jack's sermon was very well received, and many told him how it had touched them. There followed a relaxing afternoon of reading, napping, and knitting. My baby afghan is not going well, and I had to rip and start again. One of the highlights of our day is to read and answer email from family and friends. When you are so far from home, it is amazing how important that is to us, and we're not even a quarter of the way around the world yet.

Tomorrow we cross the equator with all the celebration and ritual of those of us who are "pollywogs." We have not yet crossed over to the southern hemisphere and must appease Father Neptune with sacrifice. Don't know quite what that sacrifice means, and no one will tell us. We are, however, constantly warned about the dangers of equatorial sun and must not be exposed for more than twenty minutes.

We had a wonderful dinner with our tablemates. They are delightful people whom we enjoy very much. Our entertainment tonight was a marvelous Italian tenor, Renato. Just wished he would have sung more and talked less. He is counted as one of the best tenors in the world, and we hope he will give a concert here one afternoon. Many of the artists do. We look forward to a fun and meaningful day tomorrow.

Monday, January 14: Crossed the Equator

Today was exciting. At 10:38 a.m. we crossed the centerline of the earth. We are now in the southern hemisphere. Amazing; one would expect it to be beastly hot because it is the center of the tropics. Today it was 71 degrees Fahrenheit. The sun's rays are unaffected by the tilt of the earth, so the area is always exposed to the sun and receives direct solar rays year-round regardless of the season. We learned the heat is most intense at sea level but in the mountains at the equator there can be snow. Imagine!

The legend is that overseeing the equator is King Neptune, known in Greek mythology as Poseidon, and we had a ship's ceremony to insure "safe" passage with the appearance of King Poseidon, Chief of the Water Deities. Poseidon created the horse who drew his chariot over the sea, which became smooth before him. This explains the tradition of merrymaking honoring Poseidon in return for safe passage and smooth seas.

Of course, there had to be sacrifices, and this is where the fun began. At 2:00 p.m. everyone on board gathered at the foredeck pool to witness the sacrifice of about eight crew members who had not yet crossed over. These are called "pollywogs." These poor crew members were brought in chains before King Neptune and his mermaid (babe) and his merman (Holland America is an equal opportunity ship) to be tried for their misdemeanors. It was hilarious, and when convicted they had to kiss the fish. This was a real and ugly fish—and huge! Then they were slathered all over with a white, pink, and blue foamy cream. They were then tossed in the drink (pool). It was all very festive with music, pirates, and lots of shouting and fun. We all received in our cabins a certificate of merit that we landlubbers had, indeed, crossed over.

Jack's class is going very well with fifty or more attending daily. After dinner we were entertained by Mel Mellers, a British comedian, a caustic wit very much like Dame Edna. We turn our clocks back an hour tonight. We need it as it was a tiring day.

Tuesday, January 15

Awoke to a beautiful day. At breakfast we enjoyed birds singing (recorded probably), sunshine, and sparkling water. It was heavenly. We try to breakfast alone in the dining room and we allow forty-five to fifty minutes to eat. It is right before Jack's class, and if we sit with someone, the serving takes longer, and Jack is anxious to get to his class on time. It is also a time when we share our thoughts and plans for the day as well as enjoy privately the delicious food and atmosphere.

After Jack's class, we had lunch with Father Bill, our priest, and Bob and Sheila Gan, our rabbi and his lovely wife. It is Rabbi Gan's first world cruise as well as ours, but Father Bill's had many. So we listened attentively for him to give us the "lay of the land," so to speak. We learned that we can have our laundry done free; it costs the guests $500 for the duration. However, not knowing this in advance, I did laundry today anyway as we were on phase 3 underwear. I like doing laundry and may not take full advantage of it. We can have our dry cleaning done as well. Nice! We could easily get very used to this life.

We also all spoke of ways for the three clergy to cooperate in services especially during Easter and Passover. It will be an interesting experience for all on board to see the three faiths working together. It was also suggested that they initiate a panel discussion for the guests. We are really looking forward to working closely with these clergy on board. They are great people.

It was a day of domestic tasks and emailing. Our dinner was "informal" tonight, and we simply enjoyed our table conversation. Our tablemate Jacquie is teaching us all kinds of computer skills to save on internet costs. I'm learning to cut and paste things I never knew I could.

One of the amazing things we are noticing as people confide so freely to us are the really serious physical illnesses so many people endure and yet go on with their lives. Most do so with a smile. These people are such an inspiration to us and make us ashamed to complain about anything whatsoever.

We look forward to another sea day tomorrow of living and learning.

Wednesday, January 16

It was a warmer day, at 80 degrees around 3:00 p.m. Jack's class continues to grow. Went to a port lecture on Moorea and Bora Bora. Looking forward to seeing them and just walking around these beautiful islands taking pictures and talking with the people. We arrive in Nuku Hiva on Saturday. I'm increasing my laps around the deck as my waistline increases as well. Between walking and weight lifting, I should be in better shape than at home.

With all the time changes, we're beginning to lose steam and slept soundly for two hours this afternoon. We didn't go to the theatre tonight but came to our cabin and watched a movie instead. Early bedtime sounds good. Clocks back another hour tonight. We're making about 19–20 knots and have another thousand miles before the French Polynesian Islands in just two more sea days. It's been calm and relaxing and really great, but land will look good. We are being spoiled rotten, and I think of our pilgrim families that came to the New World and traveled in horrid conditions for months and months on the ships. The *Mayflower* wasn't exactly a luxury liner. What bravery, and I have a new respect for their courage and situation.

Thursday, January 17

This is our thirteenth day at sea, and it has been wonderfully stimulating and interesting. It was even warmer today, in the eighties and beautifully clear. Jack's class was fantastic, and people are fascinated with the history, culture, and archaeology around the Bible stories. He explained the parable of the lost sheep and the fact that the lost sheep over the shepherd's shoulders was the focused image of worship for the Christians in the first three centuries rather than the cross. The cross then was a horrific means of execution until it was outlawed by Constantine in the fourth century.

I went to a port lecture about the island of Samoa and then had coffee with Sheila Gan, the rabbi's wife. She is a delightful lady, and we are enjoying getting acquainted. At dinner tonight, we learned about waterbirds that are of the pelagic groups. These are birds that never go to land, but live and breed only on the seas. The albatross is one, and the brown-toed booby (really) is another. Some of these birds have been sighted by our tablemate, who is a real birder, and when Jack has been walking on deck about 5:00 a.m., he has seen some birds that have landed on the decks. The crew carefully scoops them up and pushes them over the side rails, and they fly off. At night the ship's lights attract them. I had no idea that birds could live and not ever reach land.

We will reach Nuku Hiva on Saturday, and we have already sailed over 4,000 miles from Panama. We have only about 400 miles to go. Then the real activity and touring begins. We have made some decisions as to what land tours we wish to take and will sign up for them tomorrow. We will tour ourselves in the Polynesian islands and then take guided tours in New Zealand and Australia.

We saw a movie at the theatre tonight (this ship has everything). It was a fairy tale called *Stardust*, and it was charming. Another beautiful day is promised tomorrow, and we turn our clocks back one hour again. Soon we will meet ourselves coming, and we will be crossing the International Date Line soon.

Hello, everyone:

Here is the third installment of the journal. It was a wonderful week full of new and sometimes strange things—but most of all, new insights and meeting people we will always remember. These French Polynesian islands are very much a paradise to behold, and the dear people are mostly kind, generous, and very, very polite. It is obvious they have their problems as well. Poverty, political issues, and domestic problems are there as in any society, and they will be in our prayers now that we know them better.

We think of each of you daily and hope you will keep us in your thoughts and prayers as well. It is good to hear from home, so please email us. We get them all, and each day after lunch, we rush back to our cabin to see who has written today. In all the excitement of our adventures that is still the highlight.

Our blessings and love to each of you.

Joyce and Jack

JOURNAL # 3

The days are getting hotter as we travel farther south toward New Zealand. After class this morning we exercised and sent the second installment email of journaling. We had lunch and signed up for shore tours in New Zealand and Australia. We are hoping to be escorts for some of them.

At lunch we were told an interesting account of one couple's experience when he had a massive heart attack on board another HAL cruise. They told of the wonderful medical care and assistance they received from HAL during that experience. We learned that HAL always has a trauma doctor aboard every ship. They also stressed the importance of always having the emergency number of the port agent with you as you leave the ship. That is the second time we have heard of the excellent care someone has received in an emergency situation. It is reassuring to hear such accounts when so far from home.

We were treated to a lovely dinner in the Pinnacle Grill on ship tonight by our tablemates, Jacquie and Bob Paul, to thank us for our caring and support during their difficult time in Panama City. At that time we feared Jacquie would have to be airlifted to the States because of possible appendicitis. Thankfully, she is recovering from her abdominal infection well.

Tomorrow we dock, and we will enjoy exploring the first Polynesian island of Nuku Hiva.

Saturday, January 19

We have docked offshore after eight days at sea. Land looks really good. The Marquesas island of Nuku Hiva is very mountainous, volcanic terrain and very beautiful, with many flowering trees. The little harbor where we were tendered is lovely. There were no shore excursions because it is so small. The people are very attractive and gracious. There is no swimming because the waters are infested with sharks, but we saw many long boats with outriggers, and they are paddled like kayaks. In the little marketplace, the people make and sell beautiful wood carvings, jewelry, and paintings on fabric, and much more. They have very colorful prints, and the sea turtle is a popular motif. Several interesting stone statues around the island like short totems and they seem to be memorials. It is extremely hot (ninety degrees or above) on the island, and after an hour, we were quite anxious to return to the ship and air conditioning. The currency is French Polynesian francs. I bought a beautiful necklace of seeds for a thousand francs or US$10.

It was a restful afternoon and evening, and we saw a movie at the theatre, an animated feature that was cute. Early to bed and another sea day tomorrow.

Sunday, January 20

It is another beautiful, hot day at sea. Worship service was full again, even though "Walk for the Cure for Breast Cancer" was the same hour. Because it is the fiftieth anniversary of HAL world cruises, the goal is to raise $50,000 for breast cancer research, and we will be working toward that goal for the duration of the voyage.

There was another exciting development on board. After the service this morning, Jack was asked by the officer of personnel relations if he would hold a worship service every Sunday night for

Christian crew members. They get off work at 10:30 p.m. and the service would be at eleven. Most of the crew, being from Indonesia or the Philippines, are either Muslim or Buddhist, but there are several Christians as well. Jack was thrilled that they asked him, and even though he is usually totally out of it by eleven, he just left the cabin wide awake to have the service for them. That is remarkable in itself.

Tomorrow we dock in Papeete, Tahiti, and look forward to our adventures there. Tahiti and these South Sea islands are where the beautiful black pearls are harvested from the black-lipped oyster. It was also the home of the artist Gauguin. So it should be a great touring day. We aren't booked with a tour but will go off on our own.

Monday, January 21

What an exciting day today. Hot, hot, and beautiful with showers for about five minutes several times today. No classes when we have a shore day so we breakfasted and went ashore on the gorgeous island of Tahiti. We're in the capital city of the French Polynesians, called Papeete. We roamed through the streets of Papeete and shopped in the marketplace. It's fun to see the colorful fabrics called tapa, which is a bark of the paper mulberry tree beaten into a soft material they use for cloth. The black pearls from Tahiti are gorgeous and not black at all but beautiful shades of blue, green, and even red. Such luster they have, and they are very expensive. After the fun of shopping, we took our purchases back to the ship and had lunch.

Then we went back onshore to tour the area. We just got on a city bus. We didn't know where it was going, and the driver spoke only Tahitian and French but agreed to just let us ride his route with him for two US dollars apiece. We rode all through the city and into the countryside past some beautiful homes, churches, temples (Buddhist), and hotels. Way out along the ocean coastline and after all the passengers got off, the driver took us to the top of a mountain (very winding with no guardrails) where there was a modern hotel and showed us a magnificent view of the Tahiti coastline and harbor. This wasn't part of his route, but he just graciously did it to show us the beauty of "his" island. The people are polite and gracious beyond words. He took us back to the downtown of Papeete and smilingly waved us off the bus.

We then walked and saw public and municipal buildings and statues. Taking pictures along the way, we found a pretty little park with a stream and benches on which to rest and have a Coke. We found we were getting quite sunburned and hot, sweaty, and tired. So we made our way back "home" to the ship and collapsed. This tropical heat is really exhausting, but we feel ourselves adjusting to it. We had dinner with our friends and then came back to our cabin, where we sorted laundry to give our cabin steward in the morning. We answered email and are now getting ready for another shore day tomorrow.

I need to make a correction about the brown booby bird. I learned from our "serious" birder friend, Jacquie, that they do nest on land, and their nest is very strange. Simply on the ground they make a circle of stones. That circle *is* their nest, and if their babies stray out of that circle of stones, it is as if they have "fallen" out of the nest, and the parent birds refuse to recognize them as their own. Is there some sermonic value here somewhere? This world of ours is full of strange and wonderful things. Tomorrow, we leave Tahiti at 5:30 a.m. and cruise to Moorea in the Society Islands. It is still in the French Polynesians. Captain James Cook who discovered these islands named them Society Islands because it is where the royalty (society) had their "vacation" homes.

When Jack had his service for the Christians in the crew yesterday there were eight young men. It was a very intimate and meaningful service where each shared their joys and concerns. One young crewman who has been married only two months received an email from his young bride announcing that she is pregnant. It was a time of great rejoicing and yet sorrow where another crewman shared that his wife has cancer and asked for prayers for her. It is obvious that there is much to do on this little ship in the middle of the South Pacific Ocean which is one-third of the earth's surface. How blessed we feel to be here.

Tuesday, January 22

Another beautiful shore day, but I'm banished to our stateroom. Something is going around the ship, and I've got whatever it is, with slight flu-like symptoms. I'm not really ill but wiped out. Had breakfast in the dining room and then realized I wasn't well enough to go to shore. Jack did go and went on a tour of beautiful Moorea with about nine others in a private van with a guide. It's the greenest of all the Polynesians, and he got some great pictures. There are coral reefs here that are lovely and make for a very interesting coastline. "Bali High," from the show *South Pacific*, is here in the mist. We can see it from the ship and looked out at it during our breakfast. If one must be sick, this is a great place to do it. I just called for lunch and dinner, and within fifteen minutes each one arrived at my door. Even with a pretty little flower on the tray. Nice!

We will arrive at Bora Bora tomorrow, and I really want to go ashore. I think Robert Louis Stevenson's home is there, and I remember my *Child's Garden of Verses*. I hope I can do so. Maybe another night of good sleep will do it.

Wednesday, January 23

Awoke today feeling great and discovered I didn't have the flu at all but was dehydrated. In Tahiti the day before we had been walking around in beastly hot and humid weather, and I didn't drink enough water. I never realized even after constant warnings from the captain that dehydration would make you feel so terrible. Today, Jack and I went ashore to explore beautiful Bora Bora, and I took a large bottle of water with me. I'm fine, and Bora Bora was great.

We hired a taxi with about five others and toured the island. The coastline is a complete ring of coral reef with only one entrance into the port of Bora Bora. Consequently, the water is a gorgeous shade of bluish green seen nowhere else in the world, and it is said the lagoon is the most beautiful in the world as well. Many movies have been filmed here. We went to Bloody Mary's of *South Pacific* fame. It is now a restaurant, bar, and hotel, and the lady who owns it is depicted as the character of Bloody Mary in the show. She became very famous and very rich because of the play and movie.

The beaches are pristine and of white coral sand. The lovely coconut trees are everywhere. We learned about the coconut rat. This little rodent bores a hole in the coconut and feasts on the inside. Our driver stopped and got all of us a beautiful white flower and told us if you wear it over your right ear, you are married and not available. If over your left ear, you are not married. But if worn backwards over your ear (right or left), you are looking. Interesting! There were guns and supply depots still here from WW II. Our guide showed us stone circles that were once places of native worship and of human sacrifice. He explained that they didn't sacrifice each other, but their conquered enemies. We asked if there were weddings still performed there and he said yes, but he was married in his church. The missionaries put a stop to human sacrifice when they arrived and converted most of the people to Christianity. He had a decal on his van of a Bible, cross, and flame, and I asked him if he was Christian. He smilingly said he was and was Seventh-Day Adventist. I said I was Methodist, and he said, "Good, we are both Christians."

Another interesting fact was that there are no community

cemeteries there, but you bury your family in your own yard. Most of the houses, even the very elegant ones, had crypts and tombstones in their front yards. It also makes it impossible for the family to sell their land if their family is all buried right there.

Fortunately, Bora Bora is said to be 100 percent employed. Other islands aren't so lucky, and on islands such as Moorea or Tahiti, the best jobs are given to the French, and the native Tahitians or Mooreans cannot find employment. Consequently, there are movements to become independent from the French, and there are flags flying in some yards indicating an independent political stand. It will be interesting to follow what happens in the future. Robert Louis Stevenson's home is not in Bora Bora as I thought but in Samoa, our next island.

We came back to the ship and had a late lunch, rested, had dinner, and saw a good movie, *The Last Legion*. Then on to bed. Tomorrow is a sea day, and Jack's class begins again. It continues to maintain its numbers with more coming. Very gratifying for Jack to know he is helping others to learn the culture and history of the Bible.

Thursday, January 24

It was overcast and rainy this morning. Seems strange to even acknowledge rain when all you can see is water. It somehow doesn't matter where it is or coming from. Jack's class was really interesting, and he told what was behind the meaning of Jesus's parable of the woman and the lost coin. People are amazed and sometimes shocked at what it meant in ancient cultures. No wonder people keep returning to hear more. After class I went to the port lecture on Auckland, New Zealand, and then Jack joined me for the lecture from an anthropologist about the Polynesian people, culture, and language. It was very interesting, but so many statistics overwhelmed us. Tomorrow David Abbott, a TV and radio host, will be speaking on Samoa, and I think he will be more dynamic even with statistics. It was more restful today, and after lunch I enjoyed reading, and Jack continues to work away for his classes.

It was formal night, and the ladies' gowns are stunning. Also the officers' formal uniforms with all the gold braiding and buttons are dazzling. What fun to dress up once in a while. At dinner there was a very, very elderly gentleman guest who was in a magnificent naval formal uniform, and we were told that he is a retired naval admiral. He was gorgeous despite the fact that he was very frail. His ribbons and medals gleamed in the lights, and he walked with great pride and dignity. We then went to the theatre to hear Annette Wardell, a wonderful opera singer and star from London. It was a good day.

We set our clocks back another hour tonight and we will now be 6 hours different from US, EST. Tomorrow we will have been at sea for 3 weeks and it hardly feels like a week. We are so busy and it is still so exciting as we go from port to port. We are learning so much, and I will never see the world in the same light as I have in the past. I now see myself as part of a global people instead of just the privilege and blessings of living in the US. This is truly a life-changing experience, and I thank God every day for this opportunity.

Hello again, dear ones:

We are on our 28th day at sea. Unbelievable! It has been a great week, and now that we have reached New Zealand and then Australia, our tours will be closer together with fewer days at sea. It will certainly be busier if that's possible. We hope all of you are well and praying for us. Jack is continuing to love his teaching, and people are responding wonderfully to his classes and worship services. It's lots of hard work for him, but he is thriving.

Take care, everyone, and know we love you.

Blessings, Joyce and Jack

JOURNAL # 4

Friday, January 25

It's a very rainy and stormy day. It rained so hard we couldn't walk on deck, so I just walked the hallways for my mile and then went to the spa to lift weights. I'm working on the five-pound ones now, up from three pounds. Jack was able to walk his hour on deck at 4:00 a.m. With all the time changes, he is having trouble sleeping beyond 3:00 a.m. His class was very good, with great comments and questions. Our class members are certainly not shy. Had a restful afternoon on the computer, reading and napping. After dinner we went to a beautiful show of dancers and ballroom dancing exhibition. It was lovely.

Tomorrow, we dock at Samoa and today heard a very good lecture about Samoa and Margaret Mead's study, *Coming of Age in Samoa*. It compares the sexual morals of the young people of Samoa to Americans in the 'sixties and 'seventies. It was very enlightening. We look forward to our adventures tomorrow and hope the rain is over. We'll go ashore anyway and just take our umbrella and ponchos.

Saturday, January 26

Awoke today to a very stormy morning. The rain came down in sheets. We are in Samoa, and it's difficult to even see the island, but after breakfast we got our umbrella and ponchos and went onshore. We immediately found a taxi driver and hired him for one and a half hours. He was very nice and reasonably priced. We saw the cathedral in town which is very typical in church structure in the islands: white, with two towers and much larger than the regular churches. Very pretty and airy looking.

Went to the fruit market that was huge, flooded due to the rainy season and very crowded, as Saturday is market day in Samoa. Then to the town flea market with marvelous native crafts. Beautiful woodwork, coconut and turtle shell jewelry, and of course the tapa cloth in the island designs. Jack took lots of pictures, especially of the people. The men wear a wrapped skirt with a colorful flowered shirt over it, and they are beautiful, always with bright smiles and very friendly. We have never seen any of the children begging in the islands; they wave and smile as we pass them. It is one of the few places today where US currency is more than theirs and we bought several gifts to take home from the flea markets. We came back to the ship after going to the Robert Louis Stevenson's home and museum. It was a lovely manner house in the hills. But it was raining so hard and so crowded we were unable to see much. I was looking for the *Child's Garden of Verses* for our little grandsons, but the gift shop didn't have it. Will try at another bookstore.

After lunch, I made my first visit to the spa for a haircut and pedicure. Both ladies did a great job and I know I'll look presentable for the duration. Jack was also pleased with his haircut on board as well. The staff can have the services for half price when it is a shore day, which is nice, because the prices are so inflated.

Tomorrow in the wee hours of the morning, we will cross the International Date Line. When we awake in the morning after going to bed on Saturday night, we shall awake on Monday morning. We will lose Sunday completely. It is a very strange feeling to lose a whole day out of your life. I understand we will get it back, but only one hour at a time. We had a very official certificate waiting for us in our cabin saying that we had, indeed, given up a day for safe passage. Father Neptune is a harsh taskmaster.

Because we will not have a Sunday worship for us and the Catholics on board, we have had worship tonight at 5:00 p.m. It was very well attended, and Jack had a terrific sermon. We look forward to a wonderful day tomorrow at sea. The next day, on to Tonga.

Monday, January 28

No, I didn't forget to write an entry, but we crossed over the date line, and Sunday didn't happen. That felt strange. For that reason, Jack will be having a worship tonight at 11:00 p.m. for the crew.

A very strange thing happened to Jack this morning. At 4:30 a.m., while he was walking on deck for his exercise and prayer, he walked past a small bird huddled on the deck. It didn't seem at all afraid, and one woman actually petted it as she went by. As Jack was walking and reading in his prayer book, he noticed in the corner of his eye a huge bird flying toward him in the deck area. It had a wing span of about four feet, and he had to duck quickly or it would have flown into him. The bird landed on deck and Jack gauged it to be about one and a half feet long. He has been looking in the seabird book to try to identify it, but has not found it as yet. It sounds like this happens often, and the crew is always alert to put barriers around them and then to help them fly off again.

Jack's class was so interesting today as he talked about what Jesus meant when he said, in Matthew 5:13 (NRSV), "You are the salt of the earth," and so on. The cultural background of salt and its meaning in Bible times is fascinating. After class I went to a lecture by the pearl divers of Australia about pearls and where several kinds come from. As we saw, the black pearls come from Tahiti, the whiter ones from Australia, and the very special ones from the Akoa oyster "Mikimoto" from Japan, China, and Korea. From Australia, the queen of the pearls are gold ones from the golden-lipped oyster. They explained about "pearl" farms and how they can seed an oyster four times in its lifetime to create the gorgeous pearls from different kinds of oysters. Amazing, and no wonder they cost what they do. They also, of course, are showing the pearls in the ship's jewelry shops, and I have never seen such magnificent ones. The theme of our lovely dinner tonight was "Pearls of the South Seas," which is also the name of this part of the World Tour.

After dinner, we attended a wonderful show given by Robert Keane from New Zealand all about ragtime music and Scott Joplin, the king of ragtime. We loved the music, and he was so entertaining. We look forward to docking in the city of Nuku'alofa, Tonga. Jack and I will be escorts on the tour of the coral reefs on Kings Island in the morning; then we will be going on a tour ourselves called "The History and Highlights of Tonga." The port talk was so interesting. Now we get to explore it ourselves. It was a good day today.

Tuesday, January 29

Today is a gorgeous South Seas day. Weather was hot, hot, and steamy hot. We began at 6:30 a.m. with an early breakfast and then on to the Queen's Lounge to meet our tour group. Both Jack and I were escorts for different tour groups. The staff can volunteer for this service to be on each bus or boat, and it simply entails assisting the tour guide in every way we can, keeping our group together, answering questions such as where to find the bathrooms, and so on. We were each issued backpacks with emergency first aid kits. So we picked up our packs and water (very important after my dehydration experience) and waited for our numbers to be called to go to the tenders for going ashore. We were supposed to dock at the pier, but the water was so rough it was not safe to dock there, so we had to be tendered in. That meant all excursions were about one to two hours late. We were escorting the group to the coral island of King's Island off Tonga's city of Alofa. We got ashore and then boarded a bus to go to the king's palace. We could only take pictures at the gate as the royal family was in residence today. We then went back to the dock and boarded a small boat to take us to the island where many enjoyed the beautiful beaches and did snorkeling, scuba diving and swimming. They saw starfish and other lovely fishes including Nemo, the clown fish. We were there for about two hours and then returned to the dock to be tendered back to the ship.

Tonga is said to be the poorest of the Polynesians. About 170 islands, many not inhabited, make up Tonga, and all the land mass combined is less than the size of New York City. It is a lush island nation with very fertile soil. It is a constitutional monarchy with the king, George I, being converted by the missionaries, and practically all of Tonga is Methodist. It is a very conservative place theologically. The people are beautiful and again extremely friendly and kind. At the island, we were given a snack of fruit kabobs of locally grown fruit. It was absolutely delicious—pineapple, bananas, mango, melons, etc., all of it freshly ripe and sweet. Not at all like we get at our grocery stores at home. Tonga means "sacred garden," and indeed that is just as it looks. At the end of our tour it is our responsibility to fill out a very detailed evaluation of the tour company we used, even counting bathrooms, cleanliness, condition of the bus, ability of the guide speaking English, etc. Most people speak very good English with a gentle lilting accent. Very pleasant to hear.

Unfortunately, we got back too late to go on our own tour that we paid for. We turned in our tickets with the hope that the excursion department will have mercy and refund our money—$100. Jack reports that his worship service for the crew is growing, and even one of the officers attended. Several in the crew know him now and call out "Father Jack!" He asked them to "just call me Jack," but they said, "Oh, no, we can't do that," so Father Jack it is. He loves the crew services as the men are so genuine and have such a thirst for religion. They sing hymns in their language, and they sound beautiful with many terrific voices among them. They also use a guitar for accompaniment.

It is so great with our tablemates at dinner because we all share what we have done that day and really learn from each other. From one we learned about "flying foxes." These are huge bats that hang in the trees by day. They are considered sacred by the people and are protected. All of us came back with sunburns, and I learned that when you use bug spray (which we have to on the islands for protection) and sunscreen, the chemicals in each counteract the other and make them useless together. We will need to be more careful. It was a tiring day because of the extreme heat so all of us went back to our cabins for an early night.

We are at sea again on our way to Auckland, New Zealand. It is beyond our imaginations that we are going to this place we have only dreamed about. I think New Zealand and Australia will be one of the special highlights.

Wednesday, January 30

We are halfway to New Zealand, and it amazes me how far south New Zealand is from Australia. After class I went to a port lecture on Wellington, the capital city of New Zealand. We are looking forward to seeing this beautiful island. At lunch we met a very nice couple from Ontario. There are many people from Canada on board. This is the first cruise they have ever taken, and this is quite a large undertaking for a very first cruise.

I learned some interesting facts today. Our priest told us that two sisters from New York City are here taking their thirty-third world cruise. *Wow!* We also learned that one person brought twenty pieces of luggage. I would like to know where she put all of her clothes. Even the largest staterooms on Verandah deck 7 aren't that large. However, HAL does provide additional clothes racks if you need them. We would have to move out of our cabin if we did that. Another gentleman always brings his lazy boy recliner and another lady always brings her sewing machine. She is a quilter and sets it up in the library to work on her quilts. I have found out that HAL will arrange to have your luggage picked up from your home and delivered to your stateroom several days before the journey. For a price, of course. We have met several people who have done just that.

It is amazing to us the care the crew takes with those needing walkers, canes, wheelchairs and motorized scooters. Even when persons go on shore tours on and off the tenders as well as the ship. Physical ailments are certainly no barrier to cruising and even touring off ship. There are absolutely not many needs that cannot be met.

Jack saw another of the large birds again today and was able to see its red webbed feet as it landed on deck. He was then able to identify it as the red-footed booby. Also the very large one that he had to duck from was a frigate bird. He is so excited about learning to identify these very unusual sea birds.

After dinner tonight we saw Greg Scott a marvelous violinist from the UK. The entertainment has been first rate and continuous. We are still in awe that we are traveling around the world, and all the entertainers tell us in their shows that we are the most fortunate to be able to do so. Jack and I continue to feel we are blessed so very much that we still find it hard to comprehend. Tomorrow is another sea day, and we look so forward to each day and the opportunities and adventures it offers.

Thursday, January 31

We are in day 28 of our tour, and it seems like yesterday we boarded ship, which now feels like home. Today was a very windy, chilly day, in the 60s this morning. What a drastic change in two days' travel south to New Zealand. We arrive in Auckland at 5:30 a.m. and we go ashore at 9:00 a.m. for our tour. Jack's class was very good with lots of comments. We couldn't walk on deck because of the high winds and ocean spray that drenched the decks. So we walked the hallways instead. Went to a seminar on opals. I had no idea of the variety and to learn that 97 percent of the opals in the world come from Australia. The opal cutters of Australia are showing their opals on board, and they are spectacular. One pendant is selling for $163,000, and I heard tonight that it has been sold today. Incredible! My favorite was a mere $72,000.

At lunch we met a delightful couple from Berlin, Germany. They too are veteran world travelers. Also sat with a man who is attending Jack's class, and he said he accidentally wandered into the lounge where Jack was teaching and was so captivated that he has been back every day since. He said it really helps him to understand the Middle Eastern culture and what is happening in our world today and why. Interesting perspective on the first century culture and how much has not changed in two thousand years.

Spent most of the afternoon trying to get pictures uploaded in Snapfish with no luck. Oh well, will try again another day. Went to an excellent show tonight of the violinist Greg Scott and also the Kent ballroom dancers. Fabulous! We are very excited about being in New Zealand tomorrow. Our tour is of the highlights of Auckland and a good overview for our first trip here. It was a full day and another good one.

Hello again, everyone.

We've had a very busy and wonderful week in New Zealand and now heading for Australia. Many ports of call this week, several worship services and not as many classes. We are going to lose a few of our class members in Sydney as that completes the first leg of our world journey. However, we will probably be picking up some guests there, and hopefully some new people will attend the classes. They have been terrific and Jack is loving it.

We are also loving the experiences of seeing so much wonder in this beautiful world of ours. It certainly puts our country in perspective because we only get European CNN on our TVs. It is really interesting to watch the world keeping such close tabs on our election process and all the primaries in our US. It is a riveting experience for the rest of the world, and we had no idea it was such because it is so ordinary for us. We do live in a remarkable society even with all of our warts and problems. To say we are blessed is understating it tremendously. Hope you enjoy the #5 journal entries.

We love and miss all of you,

Joyce and Jack

JOURNAL # 5

We had a good early breakfast and then met our tour group at 9:00 a.m. We arrived in Auckland, New Zealand at 7:00 a.m. this morning, and what a clean and attractive city. The harbor is glorious, and it is called the City of Sails. We have never seen so many beautiful boats of every description nor so many marinas. It is very rich in Maori culture. The Maori are a Polynesian people who migrated to NZ many, many centuries ago.

This is the most modern city of NZ. We went ashore and got on buses to tour Auckland. We viewed magnificent vistas of the city and harbor from Mount Edin and were able to look directly into a huge volcanic crater. Inactive, of course—so much so that it was all grassy and cows were grazing along its rim. We then visited Auckland National Museum which was very well done, and we concentrated on the Maori section as these were the original indigenous people. There were amazing boats, totems, and meeting houses, all with the most intricate carvings we've ever seen. The architecture of the downtown buildings was beautiful and very unique. There was also a sky tower where people could bungee jump. No, thanks!

After four hours, we came back to the "mother" ship and had lunch. Then went back out to the Maritime Museum by the harbor. It was fascinating and because New Zealand and Sir Peter

Blake took the America's Cup from us in the 1980s, a replica of the America's Cup (only 7 in the world) was in the museum with a complete display and video of the race. I learned that America won the trophy from Britain's Queen Victoria and kept it for 130 years. Then NZ took the cup. We then got it back, and now Switzerland has it. It was exciting to see the cup even if it was a replica. The Maritime Museum too was very well done.

We came back to the ship to rest and had dinner, sharing our adventures with our tablemates. We all had different tours and it was fun to hear their stories. While having dinner, our ship left the Auckland port and as we were sailing out of port, a regatta was going on and crisscrossing in front of our ship. It was so beautiful to watch as the sun was illuminating the whole harbor. It was one of those memorable scenes that will stay with us.

Tomorrow is a sea day and another "Walk for the Cure" on deck. Jack will take part along with the other two clergy in a wreath-laying-on-water ceremony in memory of and in honor of those who have died and those who have survived victorious of breast cancer. We are continuing to walk and work toward our fiftieth anniversary goal of $50,000.

Saturday, February 2

Today was a sea day and a very rough one at that. The farther south we sail, the colder and rougher it seems to get. We are very close to the Antarctic Circle. Couldn't go on deck today for fear of being blown or washed overboard (just kidding, of course). The captain warned everyone to hold on as we move around the ship. There are railings everywhere. It's kind of fun really, and the ship is certainly rolling. After class today, Jack and the other two clergy participated in a very moving ceremony in the Walk for the Cure. Then some of the crew floated a wreath in memory of and in honor of those who have had breast cancer. There were quite a few walkers, and hopefully they made lots of money for research. This was done at the pool on the top deck. Even that was rolling and splashing.

Jack wasn't feeling up to par today and had a queasy stomach, so he lay low in our cabin and had dinner in the Lido (cafeteria) so we wouldn't expose our tablemates. We have a very busy day tomorrow, so hopefully he'll be okay by then. It was time to do domestic things tonight and press clothes. Fortunately, we have our laundry done so that saves lots of time.

We received notice in our cabins that we are unable to stop in Libya because of visa complications. I think that's a way of saying that due to possible unrest and their dislike of Americans right now, they will not grant us visas. That's too bad because Tripoli would have been really interesting to see. The port-of-call has been changed to Valletta, Malta, instead. That sounds interesting too, especially with all the Bible history in that area. We are looking forward to that port very much. It was a good day, and we can't believe we have been at sea a whole month. It has been terrific and certainly never boring.

Sunday, February 3

Today we docked in Wellington. It is called "Windy Wellington," but it was very calm and absolutely beautiful sunny weather in the 60s. We boarded our bus after being cleared for our tour and indeed went on a panoramic view of this capital city of NZ. It is a very hilly city, and our driver took us immediately to Mount Victoria. A twisty, steep climb and very scary because the roads were very narrow for our huge bus, with no guardrails and a thousand foot drop. We just closed our eyes and reminded ourselves that this is an "adventure." The summit was worth our fears as the views of the straits and sound of the division of north and south New Zealand Islands were spectacular. There was also a nice memorial to Admiral Byrd and his Antarctic team as well.

We then went to the Lady Rosewood Rose Gardens, part of the Botanical Gardens of NZ. These gardens had the most gorgeous roses and begonias imaginable and varieties beyond belief. These would match Buchart Gardens in Victoria, BC, Canada. However, it was more compact and smaller. We then viewed the "beehive" parliament building with its very controversial architecture. However, we learned the people are now quite proud of it. We then went on to Old St. Paul's Church and learned that it was the first Anglican Church in NZ. It was very charming and historic with lovely stained glass windows. The guide called it colonial Gothic, but we would call it carpenter Gothic. It had very beautiful wood everywhere. We toured most of the city and then back to the ship for lunch. Jack went back out into the city after lunch to take the tram ride up to the downtown area and take more pictures, getting a more personal feel for the city.

Today being a port day, worship was at 5:00 p.m. It was very well attended but not as well as a sea day because people were still arriving to the ship after shore excursions. However, there still were about a hundred people attending. Tonight, Jack will have services for the Philippine officers and crew at 10:00 p.m. and then at 11:00 p.m. a service for the Indonesian officers and crew. They love to sing their hymns in their own languages. It must be so hard to be so far from your home, your language, and your church and family. Yet they are so cheerful, caring, and nurturing not only to all of us but to each other. This ship is a little world unto itself, and you don't see it on short cruises. However, you certainly do knowing we are all together on this floating city for four months and usually in the middle of this huge ocean.

Tomorrow we dock at Christchurch. We're really looking forward to seeing this very British city. We haven't gone to the shows or movies in the last few days. There is so much going on, and early bedtime sounds good especially on shore days.

Monday, February 4

We awoke today to rain, heavy mist, cold and windy weather. It is about 50 degrees F. Brrr …. This is supposed to be summer in New Zealand. Jack wasn't able to get a shuttle this morning, so we waited until our tour at 1:30 p.m. after lunch to see beautiful Christchurch. Of course, the first thing a bus driver and guide does is take us directly to the highest summit in the city. In this case it was very, very high (no guardrails again), and the views of the city and harbor were spectacular. We were able to get wonderful pictures even in rainy and cold weather. We brought out our winter sweaters and coats and bundled up. This is a city of magnificent architecture and gardens. Canterbury College began in Christchurch which was settled by a group of hand-picked Anglicans to develop a settlement in a new world and to develop trade with Britain. The buildings are Gothic and gorgeous in detail. The college moved out of the city and left all of these lovely Gothic buildings. The city then created museums, art centers, restaurants, shops, and art galleries in these buildings right downtown. They did a beautiful job of it as well.

The Cathedral in the Square was lovely, but much to our disappointment, we were unable to stop there. The residential areas are very well maintained with gardens in front of the homes, and the public areas and parks are also very well kept—in pristine condition actually. A city that is beautiful and very restful feeling, clean and sparkling. We arrived at a historic home called Mona Vale which was a private home and then taken over and maintained by the city in their National Trust. There, we were treated to a "high" tea. Delicious and appreciated at 3:30 p.m.

The grounds were rambling with lovely gardens with lush foliage and trees. There is a tree called the Pohutukawa Tree, also called the Christmas Tree because it blooms at Christmas with a brilliant scarlet cluster blossom. It is only grown in New Zealand and nowhere else in the world. They are everywhere and very lush and pretty. In every part of the world there are flowers and trees that are so different from what we have in North America, yet there are some that are quite familiar. At Mona Vale there were hedges of hydrangeas of blue, pink and white—so lovely—and the Avon River flowed through with all sorts of ducks floating by and begging for goodies.

After touring through the commercial areas we arrived back to "mother" ship in time for dinner. Our tablemates didn't make it back or were too tired to come to dinner, so Jack and I dined alone and then went to a show in the theatre. Entertaining tonight was an American comedian, Frank King. A good laugh was needed after a tiring day.

Tomorrow we go to the Scottish settlement city of Dunedin. That will be fun to explore too. It was a good day, and we ate too much, but still a very good day.

Tuesday, February 5

What a fantastic day we have ahead for today. Jack and I quickly had a good breakfast then headed out to shore to the shuttle buses to take us eleven miles into Dunedin, New Zealand. *Dunedin* means Edinburgh in Gaelic, and it certainly did look like Edinburgh in Scotland. We loved it. The bus dropped us off in the Octagon which is, of course, an eight-sided city center. It was lovely on a sunny, cool day in New Zealand summer which was about 53 degrees F.

We found ourselves in front of St. Paul's Cathedral which is Anglican and very typically European. They were having a flower festival and the nave was filled with flower arrangements of all NZ flora. It was a lovely site and the cathedral itself was beautiful. We then just strolled along the Octagon as the spirit moved us into quaint shops. Many were selling gorgeous woolens of merino wool. This is the home of the merino sheep, and the wool is the finest and so soft and lightweight. Found a pharmacy, finally, to pick up some necessities and then found the First Ogato (a Maori term) Presbyterian Church that was a jewel in architecture. This is a city of unique architectural detail, and we have many, many pictures of buildings and statues. Robert Burns's statue is in the center of the Octagon.

We went back to the ship after about two hours for lunch and then met our bus for a Dunedin highlights tour with our guide. We went directly to the rail station, which took our breath away. It was the most beautiful Victorian architecture imaginable. Even the interior was perfect. There is only one other in the world that compares, and it is in Mumbai, India. We again, of course, went to the highest summit (no guardrails again) for vistas of the city and harbor and then to tour a lovely private, now city-owned, home called Oliveston built by a Jewish family (importers) in 1908. Everything in the home was the exact original. The family died out with no heirs, and the daughter willed the home and property to the city now in trust. It was a superb example of Edwardian design and architecture and such a treat to go through with a wonderfully knowledgeable docent. We drove through the university, the city downtown, and then back home to MS *Amsterdam*.

Because tomorrow is Ash Wednesday, tonight at dinner we celebrated Mardi Gras. The dining room was splendidly decorated in purple, green, and gold with balloons, streamers, beads, and masks everywhere. Our waiters and officers were dressed in opulent clothes in all these colors and were dazzling. There was then a parade of all the wait, kitchen, and chef's staff dressed in their own creations made of food and kitchen utensils. They even made masks from watermelon rinds, and each lady received a stunning feather mask to wear for the evening and to have as a keepsake. It was such fun to see and enjoy. The food was all New Orleans fare and was delicious. It was a celebration tonight, then tomorrow we receive Communion for Ash Wednesday at 9:00

a.m., and Lent begins. At the crew worship service Sunday, one of the young men said to Jack they have been on this ship for seven months and have never had Communion. Would Jack please have Communion soon? Of course, Jack agreed and will serve it to them on Sunday at their regular services, which is the soonest they could arrange it.

Tomorrow we go through the three beautiful sounds here in NZ, with Milford Sound being the last one. This is said to be the biggest attraction in NZ, and we hear it is magnificent. Narration begins at 8:00 a.m. on all decks as we pass through the sounds all day long with food and hot drinks being served on deck. We are looking forward to this exciting time. This is such an adventure.

Wednesday, February 6

Today is Ash Wednesday, and Jack had a worship service at 9:00 a.m. with Communion. It was very well attended even though we were beginning to go through the three sounds of the South Island of New Zealand. This is called the Southern Alps.

It was a day when most of us remained on deck so we wouldn't miss a thing. Our friends Bob and Jacquie from our table let me borrow their iPod to listen while walking for exercise, as I get very impatient and feel I'm wasting time just walking. Boy, I am so hooked and I thoroughly enjoyed listening to '50s and 60s rock music of all the songs Jack and I loved while dating in the '60s. How romantic! Also viewing these gorgeous sounds while walking and jiving along the decks. It was fun and distracted my mind from actually walking.

Our first sound was called Dusky Sound, and we began going through it around 10:30 a.m. Then around lunchtime we began Doubtful Sound, and then the best of all, at 2:30 p.m., was Milford Sound. To say it was breathtaking is a gross understatement. Our monstrous ship edged its way into the sound with four- to five-thousand-foot rock cliffs looming on either side of us. Our narrator said it was one of the eight wonders of the world and a World Heritage Site. It runs for over nine miles with lush rain forests. Jack saw a seal this morning, and it is said to be home to penguins and dolphins as well. Unfortunately, we didn't see any today.

We were so blessed today to have total sunshine. We therefore, have magnificent pictures of Miters Peak, said to be the tallest sea cliff in the world. There were several beautiful waterfalls as well. We decided that the world trip is worth everything it took to get here just to experience Milford Sound and all of New Zealand. It is a life-changing experience indeed.

Our table at dinner tonight was particularly fun because we haven't all been together for several days, with all of us going in different directions. So we had lots to talk about and adventures to share. This is the first of three sea days and we look forward to the relaxation after four very busy shore days. Sometimes it's too tiring to even attempt dinner in the dining room, but we all try to make the effort just to see our table friends again. We came back to the cabin after a stroll around the shops and lounges to listen to the music. Our clocks go back another hour tonight, and tomorrow Jack's class begins again. He is working constantly on this trip but loves it so much.

Thursday, February 7

Today we awoke to a very, very rough sea day. We breakfasted in the dining room with waiters dancing around to maintain their balance being very playful and pleasant about it all. This is the rough sea season in the South Seas.

Jack's class went very well with his explaining about the instance of Jesus healing the woman with the issue of blood for twelve years. There are several new people in the class, and it continues to grow as people tell others and we visit with people at lunch and breakfast and they learn about the class. There is a delightful new couple in the class who are Jewish, and they were so excited to hear about the Hebrew history and understand their feelings about blood and its sacredness. It was their first connection of that feeling and the fact that they do not hunt animals for sport. They are going to bring wonderful new insights into the class discussions, and hopefully more of our Jewish guests will attend.

We were unable to walk at all on deck and were warned to stay inside today. We couldn't even walk in the hallways because we couldn't walk two steps without holding on to the railings. This afternoon we had lunch in a very empty dining room. The "barf" bags are in racks by all the elevators, and many of us are seasick. Jack and I seem to be doing fine and haven't missed a meal.

Today a lady guest called Jack requesting a private memorial service. Her brother died while she has been on this trip. She is unable to leave the ship and wants to make formal and proper closure of his death. So Jack will be conducting his first memorial service on board tomorrow for her and her husband.

We had a very quiet afternoon not leaving our cabin, and our captain urged us to be very cautious moving around the ship. We heard disturbingly that one of our ninety-five-year-old lady guests was attempting to go out on deck while we were in very windy Auckland, and her walker and she were caught by the wind and knocked over. She broke two bones in her neck. She was taken to the Auckland hospital on a stretcher by ambulance and will remain there for six weeks. She is hoping to rejoin the ship when released. Plucky lady, I must say.

Dinner was quite exciting tonight with the ship pitching and rolling so violently with dishes, food, and glassware sliding off counters and tables onto the floor. It happened several times and caused quite a commotion of staff running to clean it all up and serve meals as well. When we came back to our cabin the fruit, flowers (our steward brings fresh ones every few days), and books were all on the floor. The bathroom medicine chest door had come open, and some things were on the floor as well. Only one glass was broken, but all else survived okay. We're still bouncing around and understand that this is just how it is so near the Antarctic this time of year.

Tomorrow is another sea day. Hopefully a little calmer but know it probably won't be until we hit Sydney, Australia on Saturday. We turn our clocks back another hour tonight. Poor Jack will probably be up at 2:00 a.m. instead of three or four.

Hi, everyone, everywhere:

Here is # 6. We continue to have a wonderful adventure and are now leaving Australia on our way to Bali in Indonesia. Most of our crew is from Bali, so there is much excitement on board for them to be seeing their families shortly, and they are counting the days. It's great to see them so excited to be home again, even if for only a day. Hopefully we'll get to meet some of their families. Hope everyone is staying warm and well in North America. It's about 80 today in Perth, Australia.

Love to each of you.

Joyce

JOURNAL # 6

Friday, February 8

Today was another rough, rough sea day. We're still in the "roaring 40s" latitudes where a belt of westerly winds sweeps across the southern oceans with no land mass to break up the wind. Very typical weather for February. We're approaching the southern autumn and hurricane season as well. Sure hope we can avoid them this trip. We did lie low in our cabins after Jack's class. There were over sixty people today, and we will sadly lose four or five members that leave us in Sydney. We will miss them. Especially a young man named Franko, born in Italy and living with his wife in a monastery in Canada. He is a teacher and a very intelligent and interesting man who made wonderful comments in class.

I attended the port lecture on Melbourne, Australia, and look forward to seeing this beautiful city. Then I attended another lecture about the Pacific Theatre in WWII and Australia's part in the war. I'm afraid we don't think of "down under" and the contributions these countries made and make in our world history. It was a very good lecture. Spent the rest of the afternoon on the computer and reading quietly.

We turned in early tonight. We dock at 6:00 a.m. tomorrow and will tour Sydney. Looking so forward to seeing this magnificent harbor and Opera House as we sail into port.

Saturday, February 9

We awoke this morning and opened our drapes to see the glorious Sydney Opera House out of our cabin window. We were in the famous Sydney Harbour, and it is indeed the most beautiful harbor in the world. We had a quick breakfast, met our tour bus at 8:30 a.m. and went off to see Sydney, Australia. A dream come true. It was raining like crazy, but it didn't matter.

We forget that in Sydney's history this is where England sent all of its convicts. Of course, some were only here because they stole a loaf of bread to keep their family from starvation. A penal colony is a strong influence here, especially in the buildings and churches. The buildings are lovely in a gold sandstone and great detail work. There are also much that is modern in architecture as well with skyscrapers, etc. We saw parliament buildings, churches, and commercial and residential areas. The botanical gardens were lush and beautiful as always in summer. It was a highlights tour, and that's exactly true. It just featured the highlights of this beautiful city. After three hours we came back to the ship for lunch. Again, ate quickly as we were anxious to go back out to explore on our own.

We found a taxi and went to Darling Harbour and their famous aquarium. It is a very popular family destination. We enjoyed strolling through the aquarium that is world-renowned and saw marvelous species of southern hemisphere marine life with beautiful coral, as the Great Barrier Reef is right off the coast of northeast Australia. Fur seals, sharks, stingrays of all kinds, Nemo (little clown fish) and Dory (the cute blue fish), sea horses, sea turtles, crocodiles, and my favorite, a real duck-billed platypus. It is one of the finest aquariums in the world, and we loved it. When we came out three hours later, the sun had come out and it was really hot and truly summertime.

In the morning during our tour, we went through China town and saw that today is the Chinese New Year with all the street festivities. We knew we couldn't go back by cab and be back to the ship in time for dinner, because the traffic would be impossible. We decided to enjoy another hour of strolling around this busy harbor and wait for a water taxi to take us just a few short blocks from our ship. We were able to walk through a lovely arcade area called The Rocks with shops of every description. It was all very upscale and charming.

As we sat at our table for dinner, we looked out over Sydney Harbour with a panoramic view of the city, the Opera House and the famous "Coat Hanger" bridge. That's what the Australians call the Sydney Bridge because it does look just like a coat hanger. It is the widest long-span bridge and the highest in the world. One of our tours offered was to climb to the top of the bridge and down again—with supports, of course. Some of our guests did just that. It not a pretty bridge but very impressive.

The Sydney region has been populated with the indigenous Australians, called Aboriginals, for over forty thousand years, and many of their rock carvings and names of areas are around the city. Australia, we learned, is the oldest continent of all our continents. A little fact: when we reached Sydney, our ship had traveled 11,399 miles from Fort Lauderdale, Florida. Incredible! Happily, we will be here another day, and tomorrow we will tour the Opera House in the morning and go off on our own in the afternoon. Tomorrow promises to be a sunny, warm, beautiful day.

Sunday, February 10

Yes, today is a gloriously sunny and warm day. Summer clothes have come out again all over the ship. After breakfast we joined another tour group for exploring the Opera House. It is one of the most amazing architectural structures imaginable. It is world-renowned with its magnificent sails of tiles on the roofs. It was built thirty-four years ago, in the 1970s, by a Danish architect.

It was supposed to be built in two years at a cost of $7 million. Because of the quagmire of politics and the fact that no one could figure out, including the architect, how to construct the roof line, it took fourteen years to build, at a cost of $102 million. The city of Sydney decided to create a lottery to pay for these enormous overruns and were able to completely pay it off in eighteen months. This is staggering, indeed.

We were able to go up the 200+ steps to go into the opera theatre and the concert hall. There are five venues in the Opera House, and actually it is a complete arts center. Five performances can occur at one time. One theatre was built to house opera and ballet. The acoustics were perfect and the ceiling was constructed like the roof of one's mouth. The sound is so perfect that there is no amplification at all. It is the same in the concert hall where the symphony and all musical and theatrical performances are held. It is in the round with audience seating behind the orchestra as well as in front. The ceiling there is conical in design and again perfect for sound in that venue. The Opera House is a World Heritage Site, which is extremely rare because it is only thirty-four years old, and also the architect is still living. I will never forget the feel of walking through that incredible structure. Sydney and all of Australia is very proud of this now famous landmark.

We then boarded our bus for a second tour of the city and especially the famous Bondi Beach. It is on the Tasman Sea, and the surf and waves were tremendous. We happened to be there just as the 2008 Australian Ocean Swim was going on. It is a national meet of expert swimmers who are taken out about two kilometers and then swim back to shore. To look at those waves and turbulence of the sea, you would think them crazy. But many did swim it and strangely but importantly, the rescue workers were all around them in rubber motorboats to chase away the sharks, as the waters off Sydney's coast are infested. They are also there to assist the swimmers if they run into trouble. The coastline is very popular with surfers worldwide, and I think everyone was there today.

We came back to the ship for a late lunch, and then Jack and I walked up to the shopping area of Sydney about a half-mile from our port dock. Here, it is a shopper's paradise. I was able to find a pharmacy to buy pantyhose (desperately needed). We found gifts and walked through a wonderful outdoor market in "The Rocks." This was the penal colony area. We bought a lovely matted photo of Sydney Harbour and Opera House. We came back early because worship was at 5:00 p.m. today since we are in port. It was surprisingly well attended especially since we didn't have to be back on ship until 10:30 p.m. tonight. Jack is now at the two services for the crew. One is at ten, and one at 11:00 p.m.

It is now 11:00 p.m., and I just began to feel the ship leaving Sydney Harbour. As I look out our cabin window, I can see the city and harbor lights fading. I leave with a little sadness and pray we can return to Sydney again. It is beautiful and the people so gracious. We sail for a day and then dock at Melbourne. We look forward to that port and new experiences there. Jack's class begins again tomorrow. It will be another beautiful day.

Monday, February 11

Today was a sunny and warm sea day. Jack's class was quite full. We were sad to see several of our members leave us in Sydney, but more joined us, and there were about seventy-five people attending. Jack gave the first of several lectures on forgiveness and traced the development of the concept of forgiveness into the New Testament. A fascinating subject.

I exercised on deck with the trusty iPod (which I adore, by the way) and lifted my weights. I'm now up to five pounds. With all we've been eating, I need more than this. The meals are so wonderful, it's easy to overeat severely. It was a quiet afternoon of reading, writing on the computer, and napping. We've had two very tiring days, and today was a good balance of relaxation. Went to the port lecture on Fremantle and Perth, and look forward to experiencing the totally different typography of these, our last ports in Australia.

We all made it to our dinner table tonight, and it was fun sharing our different experiences in Sydney. We later viewed the award-winning *La Vie en Rose*, featuring a look at the life of Edith Piaf. It was very well done and certainly deserved all the awards, but what a tragic and torturous life she had. Tomorrow we dock at 5:00 a.m. in Melbourne, and we have a tour on the Puffing Billy train into the countryside and the Dandenong Ranges. It will be our first other than highlights tour, and we hope to see some real Australian wildlife. We enjoyed the quietness of today.

Tuesday, February 12

Today we toured Melbourne, the second largest city of Australia. Had a good hot breakfast, then off for adventure. We traveled about an hour from port to board the Puffing Billy Tour Train to view the Dandenong Ranges. Melbourne is rather flat, so this 1800-foot elevation was the peak of Melbourne in the small town of Belgrave. Very pretty, lush and rain forest type countryside and beautiful fern trees. We think of ferns as plants, but these grow as large as trees. We saw several cockatoos in the trees with very loud calls. They were bright white and very large birds with that pretty top plume.

We then went to the top overlook of Dandenong Mountain. Unfortunately, it was rather foggy so our aerial photos probably won't be as good; but they did have lovely gardens with a nice variety of flowers and plants. This is the home of the kookaburra as "in the old gum tree." We saw many gum and eucalyptus trees but no kookaburra birds.

Melbourne is a modern city that looks very much like Chicago. It was built from a "gold rush" economy in the 1800s. It also, again, was a penal colony with the convicts building a great deal of the old city with that beautiful gold sandstone and black volcanic stone. The picturesque Yarra River runs through the city with many peaceful-looking gardens and parks throughout, and the cutest trams run all over the city. This is also the premier wine region for Australia.

We came back quite late for lunch and didn't have enough time to go back out to explore because we were scheduled to set sail at 6:00 p.m. We did so as we had dinner and again had a most gorgeous panoramic view of Melbourne harbor while sailing off into the sunset.

Jack and I attended the show tonight of Soul Mystique. They are a beautiful and talented couple who are the Australian ballroom dance champions. They not only danced stunningly but were quick-change artists as well. It was a fun performance, and the costumes were magnificent. We are leaving the Tasman Sea between Tasmania and Melbourne and entering into the Indian Ocean. I love the exotic names of all these places. We will sail for three days to get to Perth on the southwest corner of Australia. Jack's class begins again tomorrow. It promises to be another beautiful day.

Wednesday, February 13

Today was a cold, windy, and very rough sea day. Not what we expected. Many of our friends and classmates have terrible head colds, so Jack and I have started taking our Airborne three times a day to hopefully avoid it or at least have a milder case. One half of our table are banished to their cabins so as not to spread it around. However, we're hearing lots of coughing and sneezes in class. Our new Jewish couple is enjoying the class and excited to learn about our joint heritage that they never knew or understood before. New people are coming by hearing from others. It's a blessing to see the hunger people have to understand the Bible. Jack and the other two clergy will be interviewed tomorrow, on Valentine's Day, about weddings and funny romantic stories they have about their wedding experiences. It will also be televised ship-wide, so it'll be fun to watch.

At lunch today, we met a dear lady who is traveling alone. This is her ninety-first cruise, many of them world cruises. Her husband died just this year, but she decided to come anyway. Dear friends meet year after year on this particular cruise, and she is comfortable traveling even under her circumstances. She is so brave to do this in her bereavement.

There is a great excitement among the crew members because after our port of Perth, we travel to Bali in Indonesia and to the Philippines and they will again see their wives, parents, and children. Many of the families will come on board to tour the ship and see their spouses or children who work so tirelessly for us. One of our favorite waiters told us this is his last year on HAL. He has made enough money with HAL to now go home and start his own business. They are such ambitious and hardworking people.

I went to a seminar on coral and pink diamonds this morning. These diamonds are the rarest in the world, and 95 percent are minded in Kimberly Mines, northwest Australia, and the other 5 percent in Africa. They are so rare that they are actually museum pieces and cost one million dollars per carat. Imagine! They are being displayed on ship, and they do have some of them for sale. You can be sure they will sell some of them, as they are gorgeous.

After dinner tonight Jack and I went to the theatre to see a young flautist, Clare Langan. It was the finest and most beautiful flute music I have ever heard. She is world class and has performed for the royal families often. She is British and dazzling.

Tomorrow is another sea day and promises to be just as rough going. The barf bags are back in the elevator racks. That is always an indication of the condition of the ship's passengers. I hear we have a regular seasick menu that consists of a ginger drink, green apples, and grilled chicken breasts. Hope it works. However, Jack and I are still doing fine and sleep like babies in a rocking cradle.

Thursday, February 14 – Valentine's Day

What a fun day this is. After breakfast I went to Jack's class, which was fascinating. We're still on forgiveness. We met a man in our hallway who said, "You know, I go to the Catholic service, the Jewish Sabbath Eve Service, and your Protestants' service, and there's great similarity in all of you." He's right. We're all about God's love.

After class Jack and the other two clergy were interviewed by Jackie, our social hostess on board, and she had them talk about weddings at which they have officiated and other romantic stories. Then she had Jack and Rabbi Bob tell about their own weddings. It was a hilarious time, and about 200 people came to the interview. I have to admit, I did hold my breath wondering what Jack would talk about. Of course, he told about my being a half hour late for our wedding, much to the amusement of the audience. It was all in fun, and folks loved it all. After the "coffee chat," as it's called, we had lunch with Rabbi Bob and Sheila, his wife. They are delightful people. We are getting better acquainted but don't get to be together often. We're all so busy doing our own thing with the groups we're here to serve, and the days fly by.

We had a delicious dinner tonight, special for Valentine's Day, and the dining room was ablaze with red and white streamers, heart balloons, and beautiful hangings from two stories up. It was stunning, and of course, the officers and waiters were dressed in red-and-white spangled outfits. It was the prettiest of all the decorations we've had so far. After dinner, Jack and I were invited to a Valentine's Day party in the Crow's Nest given by two delightful ladies who are sisters. The total staff was invited as well as many, many guests. The other day we found a beautifully engraved invitation at our door for the party, and Father Bill (who comes almost every world cruise and knows these things) told us that these ladies from Florida have this spectacular party every year in appreciation for all of us. The food and drinks were amazing, and the ladies graciously greeted all of us at the door. It was lovely, and there had to have been three or four hundred guests present. We heard these ladies each have a cabin with a cabin between them just for their clothes. Another lady provides a party on the Lido deck for the whole crew at another time when the crew is off. Amazing! There are about five hundred crew members.

Jack and I spoke to a few people we knew and then left to go to the show at the theatre. We saw Annie Frances, a young Australian singer who sang folk, country, Broadway, and some multilingual classics. They were beautiful. She told that her mother is Philippine and her father is Irish, and when she sang a very poignant Irish song about the prison ships sailing to Australia from Ireland, I realized fully that this continent was developed on the shoulders of much heartbreak. Prison labor built these beautiful buildings and cities, and the prisoners were separated from their families often because they only stole food for their children. What cruelty. The British also treated the Aboriginals so abusively, separating children from their parents to put them in institutions. Reminded me of our treatment of our Native Americans. Only yesterday on CNN we saw where Australia apologized publicly and politically for the abuses to the Aboriginals. Maybe we are growing?

We are still meeting new people at breakfasts and lunches and being able to call people by name now. We feel we are very fortunate to be here doing this. We turn our clocks back another hour tonight. We are now ten hours distant from EST, USA, and now I can see that we will get our day back that we lost crossing the Date Line. Another sea day tomorrow with other adventures. Things to learn and people to meet.

Hello again, everyone:

This was a very interesting week with our stops at Perth and Bali. I'm still fighting this cold but getting better each day. Fortunately, Jack hasn't gotten it yet, and hopefully he won't. He's the one that has to keep up the pace. We have lots of time for relaxing in the afternoons, except on Sundays when we're at port, of course. Those days are exhausting for Jack, and he rests the next few days to catch up again. The crew and guests are a delight, and we're having a good time with everyone we meet.

We've had both calm and very rough seas and even a scare of a cyclone, which our wonderful captain avoided, thank God. Our destination is Brunei on Borneo Island, and we shall arrive there on Sunday. We miss all of you and hope you are well and staying warm this winter. Can't believe that we have just avoided winter completely this year and will pick up spring when we return. We haven't hit our halfway mark yet but will do so in Hong Kong. It has been such a thrill.

Love to all of you,

Joyce and Jack

JOURNAL # 7

Friday, February 15

Well, no surprise. I have whatever is going around the ship—a bad head cold. I have to admit it's rather nice if one must be sick to just lie here and have my meals delivered even with a pretty flower on my tray. Tomorrow we dock in Fremantle and Perth. We had planned to tour Perth with a river cruise down the Swan River (this is famous for the black swans swimming by) but decided we should redeem our tickets and Jack will explore the small town of Fremantle where our ship will be moored. We hear it is a lovely little town full of quaint shops. I probably should stay put in our cabin and not expose anyone else. Illness spreads like wildfire on ship. I'm disappointed, but Jack promises to take lots of pictures for me to see what I'm missing. When we leave Perth tomorrow, we head out to the Indian Ocean on our way to Bali. To bed early tonight with the hope of feeling better tomorrow.

Saturday, February 16

It is a beautiful hot summer day in Perth. We docked about 7:00 a.m. I still have my cold and stayed in the cabin until about 9:30 a.m. I went to breakfast in the Lido, and Jack went onshore. We docked in the port of Fremantle, and those on tour took buses into

Perth several miles away. Because we redeemed our tour tickets and someone else on the waiting list snapped them up quickly, Jack just walked around the pretty little town with its many old shops. I amused myself by sitting placidly in a deck chair reading and doing Sudoku.

This is the area of diamond mines—mostly industrial diamonds and a few gemstones, especially the famous pink diamonds. It is also where gold mines are located, and because of this, it is a very wealthy area. Just outside the city is where the desert begins. Australia has a very low population outside of the cities along the coastline. The interior is very wild and not very habitable. We are getting closer to the equator, and it's getting hotter. Jack came back at lunchtime just drenched and had to shower and change his clothes.

This evening for dinner we were treated to an Australian BBQ. Of course, the food was spectacular, and a band called the Windjammers from western Australia (southwestern actually) performed. They were lots of fun with their striking accents. They sang sea shanties, Australian folk songs like Waltzing Matilda, and country-westerns from the US. They were quite good, and they brought their families on board to join us. It was a really good time for all of us. I'm beginning to feel better and go out a bit more without feeling I'm contaminating the ship.

Tomorrow is Sunday, and we are heading out to the Indian Ocean for three days at sea to dock at Bali. Really looking forward to this exotic port. All our lives we have heard these beautiful and exotic names. I can't believe that we will actually see them and talk with the people who live there. This is truly a blessing.

Sunday, February 17

Today was another beautiful sunny day at sea, calm in the morning. Jack reports it was a full house at worship today. I stayed in for another day of recovery. I'm doing well and think I can go back to regular routine tomorrow.

We had lunch today with Father Bill, and he told us that the cruise director wants to have an Easter sunrise service on ship. That will mean four services that day for Jack. Poor guy. Well, he says that's why we're here. This is no job for sissies, believe me. He knows this is a way to spread the gospel in a whole new way. It's exciting for both of us to see how people respond, knowing we will be together as a congregation for only four months. It's like they want to cram it all in at once. The thrill of this adventure is like a mountaintop experience for all of us, with all of our senses heightened and our spirits challenged in many ways. I only pray it will continue for folks to seek more in their home churches and that this is just the beginning of even more growth.

We were all able to meet tonight for dinner together. We enjoy our table friends so much. Each couple is quite different, and each person adds a great deal to our collective friendship. They are wonderful, and we look forward to dinner together each evening.

Our captain warned us tonight that we are heading for a cyclone off the coast of Australia, and the crew is battening down the hatches on deck. He asked that we not go on deck tomorrow, as forty-mph winds are expected, with rough seas ahead. Looks like the barf bags come out again. Captain promises to keep us far from the eye, but I'm sure we'll have some of it by morning. Hope we can get to class because Jack is beginning the parable of the lost son. This has to be my favorite parable. Jack is now at the 11:00 p.m. service for crew members, and hopefully tomorrow will be calmer than expected.

Monday, February 18

Wow! We didn't get nearly the high seas we expected. Just moderately rough today but hot, humid and cloudy. Our captain has successfully skirted around the cyclone, Nicholas. So we all breathed a great sigh of relief. Jack's class was very interesting, and he began the first lecture on the prodigal. People can't wait for the next episode tomorrow. Today he told about the family structure and inheritance laws of Bible times. Those forty-five minutes of class fly by quickly. We had a quiet afternoon receiving and answering email and reading. Dinner tonight was formal and then an evening of entertainment with Annie Frances, the lovely singer and Dave Levesque, a wonderfully funny violinist and comedian.

I attended a port lecture on Brunei, which is our port after Bali. Brunei is on the island of Borneo. This sounds so mysterious. As we head up into Indonesia and Borneo, I can't help singing songs from *The King and I*. The pictures of the temples look so tantalizing, and it's truly a thrill to actually see them. It was a very good day, and I'm recuperating well. Needed to rest this afternoon. Tomorrow will be better.

Tuesday, February 19

Today began a sunny, sparkling sea day, but as it progressed, we ran into clouds and rain. Jack's class was fascinating, and people were astounded as he gave the second lecture of the prodigal: where he went, what his temptations were in a modern Greek city, and why he couldn't go home again.

After class we had cappuccino with Jacquie and Bob, our good table friends, and then I went to the lecture by Aileen Bridgewater about Hong Kong. Unfortunately, we didn't learn much about Hong Kong; because she was a talk-show hostess on radio there for seventeen years, she told mostly about famous people she had interviewed. It was gossipy and interesting but disappointing. I'm afraid I'll have to wait for our port guide Barbara's lecture on Hong Kong. She is a wonderful lecturer and very helpful guide.

We had a quiet afternoon reading and resting, and it seems I am still recouping from my cold. Tomorrow we dock at Bali. The excitement on ship is electric, especially among our crew. After a great dinner, Jack and I went to a movie called *I Now Pronounce You Chuck & Larry*. It was very funny, and a good laugh sure helps digestion. Home to bed and ready for a big tour day tomorrow.

Wednesday, February 20

What a day this was! We arose at 6:30 a.m. to be ready for our tender into Bali leaving at 9:00 a.m. It took about thirty to forty minutes by boat to reach the gorgeous port of Padang Bay, Bali, which is our first port in Indonesia. As we disembarked from the tender, there was a feast for our eyes, ears, and all senses. There was a huge sign welcoming our Golden Odyssey World Cruise with red carpets laid on the dock for us. The dock was lined with lavish drapings and hanging ornaments and colorful fringed umbrellas along the path. Then there were beautiful young Indonesian girls dressed in native gold and red dresses and headpieces dancing to the music of a gold and red garbed orchestra seated on the ground under a tent close by. The music was a rhythmic beat with what sounded like xylophones or marimbas. It was so awesome that most of us had tears in our eyes because of their graciousness and obvious joy of our coming to Bali. They do have a good tourist trade, but few cruise ships come here.

That was our official greeting, and then we turned around and saw the people of Bali behind barriers waiting for us to come onto our buses. They descended on us in droves, selling all the typical Indonesian wares of postcards, fabrics of gorgeous designs, wood carvings, metalwork, puppets, beads, and silver. This was our first encounter with Far Eastern hawkers. It was daunting to be sure, and I certainly have much to learn in the bartering method. I soon learned they have little respect for you if you just give them their first price, which can be exorbitant. I looked at the poverty of those people, and it was all I could do not to just hand them what they asked for. What especially wrenched me were the little girls, some only three or four years old, who would just walk up to you and hand you a flower that they had obviously picked off a nearby bush and then with darling liquid brown eyes plead for a dollar. Our friends are trying to harden me, but I don't know if that will happen.

Our first stop was to a tenth-century Hindu temple and Museum of Semarajaya. It was unbelievable in design and sculpture, with artwork even on the ceilings. These structures are all outdoors and looked like pavilions in a temple courtyard. This was our first experience of Hindu culture, and about 90 percent of the Balinese people are Hindu. Out of respect we were required to wrap a tablecloth-length cloth around our waists to our knees. The gardens and pools were lovely, and there was a fenced-in area more ornate. Fringed umbrellas were set around the altar area, which was the holy of holies, and on the gate was a sign saying what one cannot bring into the holy area. It said in bold letters that a woman who is menstruating cannot enter. Wow!—right out of Bible times, when women on their period were unclean. Jack had to have a picture of that sign for his lectures. We had a peaceful half hour there, and then we were ushered back to our buses; to get there, we had to just put our heads down and rush through the crowd of hawkers.

We then drove through the city of Bangli, a more affluent community, and they call it the city of a thousand temples. Indeed, that's just what it was. Each family has their own small yard with a very well kept area fenced or walled off for their temple. Each temple had four or five shrines in it. The rest of the yard might be a trash heap, but that part is lovely with flowers, a little bowl of rice, and incense as well. The people have three temples: their home temple, the community temple, and a "functional" temple. The functional temples are in the workplace, rice paddies, and farmlands.

We drove through many miles of countryside. We saw magnificent sites of rice paddies full of water, terraced fields, farmlands, water buffalo, and women carrying wood or anything else on their heads. One man was carrying a load of bricks on his head with no hands. We saw many people working in the rice paddies in water up to their knees. Rice crops can be harvested two or three times a year depending on the type of rice grown. That and tourism are their main economic sources. Our guide said many of their young people leave the farm for other jobs so they don't have to work in the rice paddies, which can cause many health problems.

We stopped at another Hindu temple at the top of hundreds of steps. You could actually take good pictures from the bottom, so Jack and I stayed there. To go up one must "rent" a temple sash for your waist. As we were standing there a young man and Jack began talking. The man was the keeper of the temple, and Jack learned that the priest comes only twice a year. There are ceremonies that occur such as births, marriages, an old-age ceremony, and death. They talked for quite a while, and then he turned to Jack and said, "Of course, you have a donation for the temple and also for myself?" We had to laugh, and naturally Jack offered a donation, which was happily accepted. There were also hawkers there, but as long as you stayed on the bottom step of the temple steps, they didn't approach you. Aha!

We then drove to Mount Batur, the highest point of Bali. Again, no guardrails; the driver drove this huge bus like a maniac, and of course everything deferred to this monster bus on the road. I didn't dare look out my window because I knew it was a sheer drop-off. My prayers have never been so graphic. When we reached the top of Mount Batur, there was a beautiful Indonesian restaurant waiting for us with a sumptuous buffet of all native food and spotlessly clean restrooms. This was truly worth the ride up, and the view over the rice paddies and ponds was stunning. Everything is so green and lush because of the rain forest. However, as we left our buses, there were the same hawkers we left at the last temple. We all looked at each other and decided they must have hung on to the back of the bus, or they knew a back way up the mountain—amazing! I think people bought things because they were so impressed with their tenacity.

After lunch, we went to the town of Tenganan, an artesian colony with very primitive shops and saw some really lovely things. Jack bought gorgeous painted eggs from two very young artists. I bought gold and brown fabric and silver bracelets. We then came back to the port in pouring, drenching rain to await our tender back "home." It seems the more foreign and unusual our tour, the more we look at the MS *Amsterdam* affectionately as "home."

We were late for dinner at our table in the dining room and went instead to the Lido. We ate quickly and crawled back to our cabin for showers and bed. Tomorrow we're anxious to hear from Zulu, our cabin steward, and Asep, our waiter, about their visits with their families. This day was the most adventurous so far.

Thursday, February 21

Today, was a good day to rest. None of us moved too swiftly after our long day yesterday. It was nasty outdoors but hot, humid, and cloudy. Seas were calmer than we've had in a while.

Many of our crew seemed really happy to have been home for a day at least. Zulu, our cabin steward, told us that thirteen members of his family came on board to visit him and tour the ship. After seeing the poverty of Bali, we would venture to say that he is probably contributing to the support of his entire family. Asep, our very handsome young waiter, told us that several members of his family came on board. He was thrilled especially to be with his wife and little four-year-old daughter. His eyes sparkle when he talks about them. He said they were in awe of the ship and took many, many pictures to share with other families.

We heard there were over a thousand visitors to the ship that day and I'm sure lunch was served to all our crew's families. How difficult it must be to be separated, but how fortunate for them if they are selected to work on board the ships. It must be a precious few. When we reach Manila in the Philippines, more of our crew will visit with their families.

Jack's class was really good today, and we have a faithful group. Regardless of other activities, they are there and want to talk afterwards. Went to a port lecture today on Manila, and it sounds wonderful. We rested and read this afternoon and then went to dinner tonight. It was fun to talk with our friends about our different experiences on Bali and what we bought from the hawkers and shops. Tomorrow night is the captain's elegant formal dinner, but the next night we are all going to bring our purchases to dinner for show-and-tell and the circumstances under which we bought them. Each will be fun, I'm sure. Came back to the cabin early tonight just to read and relax. We find pacing ourselves is necessary. Look forward to another good day tomorrow.

Hi again, everyone:

It was an extremely interesting and busy week seeing Brunei, Manila, and Hong Kong. Today we are in Vietnam and have three days here. I must say it is beautiful countryside and harbors, and I can see why this is the number-one destination for vacations in the world today. This fact amazed both of us, but we now understand why construction of hotels, restaurants, and apartment complexes is everywhere.

Jack's classes continue to be very well received, and more than seventy-five people attend every day we are at sea. This has been an incredible journey, and what an adventure. We are halfway around the world now in China and Vietnam, with another half of the world to go. We are hoping it doesn't go too fast, but I can see where it may because of all the ports ahead. There is also so much to do on the ship that you can't possibly do all you would like to. But the people, the people are why we are here, and they are just wonderful. We are so happy and feel so blessed.

We love you all and will see you in another two months.

Jack and Joyce

JOURNAL # 8

Jack is now coming down with this awful cold we are passing around. We're hoping he will be well enough to go to class tomorrow. We'll see. I'm doctoring him up with Airborne, Zicam, Nasonex, and Tylenol. He's coughing and sneezing away in bed right now. Thank goodness, he doesn't have far to go for anything.

After a wonderful class today, I went to a lecture on Fabergé eggs given by our manager of the Merabella Jewelry Center. This is the really exclusive, pricey jewelry store on board. It was so interesting as he told the history of the Fabergé family being exiled from France due to religious persecution. They were Huguenots, and they finally settled in St. Petersburg, Russia. They then became the jeweler to the czar. For an Easter gift, the czar gave the czarina an egg made of wood, painted with a special enamel and gold with a surprise inside. First a gold ball, and inside was a chicken, and inside that a Russian diamond. The czarina was so thrilled with this that she wanted one every year. So they commissioned the Fabergé family to make them.

The egg symbolized rebirth, strength, and new life and is found in many religions and celebrations. These were called imperial eggs because they were made for the czar or made only for royalty. The British royalty have a large collection of them. Also the king of Thailand and now the Forbes family in the US collect them. There are only ten places in the world where they can be seen, and this ship is one on this grand world cruise. They have brought on board the Petersburg Collection, which is spectacular, and the shop is like a museum, they are displayed so beautifully. They start at five thousand dollars. Jack and I just went this morning for a showing, and people were buying them like they cost ten dollars instead of a king's ransom. Robert, the manager told us they will sell them all before we reach Russia. Amazing! We just wanted to go and feast our eyes on their beauty. There is still one family member, Sarah Fabergé, who is making them, but there were also some in the shop that her father, Theodore, had made much earlier.

After lunch was a restful time of emailing and reading. There was a lovely captain's formal dinner tonight, and we were all given commemorative plates at our setting for the occasion and this voyage. It will certainly have a place of honor in our china cabinet. Barbara, our port lecturer and guide, sat at our table this evening, and she was a delight. Her knowledge of what to do and see around the world is remarkable, and she is the best port guide we've ever experienced in traveling. After dinner I brought Jack back to the cabin and tucked him in with a large box of Kleenex and his Vicks. Tomorrow is another sea day and more to learn and do.

Saturday, February 23

It was a lovely sea day today. The sun shone, and it was warm and breezy out on deck. Jack felt better today, having slept well, and went off to class. I, however, needed a down day and slept until nine o'clock. Felt good.

I was in a deck chair this morning just reading and looking out at the beautiful blue South China Sea, and Mary, one of our class members, came by my chair, and stopped. She said she missed me in class and I told her I needed a morning not having to be somewhere, and she began telling me how very grateful she is to be in Jack's class. It seems that she's realized for the first time what real "salvation" means. Jack explained that it is the moment when you first accept that you are accepted by God. She explained that she teaches a Bible study in Las Vegas and many of her class members are showgirls or others whose lives are less than holy, and now she understands what she can tell them because they say, "But, Mary, you don't know what I have done in my life." She said that now she can say she knows it doesn't matter. "God loves and accepts you anyway." Mary is a devoted Roman Catholic and goes to the Catholic mass every morning and Jack's class right afterward. She is from Egypt, speaks with a beautiful accent, and is a very unusual and lovely lady. I have to admit I sat for about five minutes with tears in my eyes. It touched me so very much. We've learned that several of our class members teach Bible classes in their churches, and I see them taking notes furiously. After lunch we rested so Jack can recoup for tomorrow's worship services.

We are now traveling up the coast of Malaysia in the South China Sea, and we will dock in Brunei, Borneo island, our second Indonesian stop, at 6:00 a.m. We have a tour at 8:15 p.m. on the splendors of Bandar, the capitol of Brunei. We've very excited to explore this beautiful kingdom. It is a Muslim nation, led by a Sultan, and is an extremely wealthy country thanks to offshore oil and natural gas. We've been given all kinds of instructions of what not to wear and the etiquette of Brunei. We came back to our cabin right after dinner to get ready for our exciting adventure tomorrow.

Sunday, February 24

Today was incredible. We docked at 7:00 a.m. in Bandar, Brunei. Borneo is the island where tribal headhunters would display the heads of their enemies. Goodness! We had a wonderful guide who spoke beautiful English, so we were able to follow him very well as we learned about Brunei, Islam, and the sultan. Jack and I couldn't believe there are still places such as this in the world. It is a kingdom with a sultan/king and is an absolute monarchy. They are exceedingly rich with vast oil and natural gas wealth. There is no income tax of any kind, and education is free, even if one wishes to go to college abroad. Health care is free, and their hospital is beautiful. They pay one dollar for everything. The petrol costs $1.50 a gallon. There is probably a waiting list to come into the country. However, it is 90 percent Muslim with gorgeous mosques everywhere and magnificent homes, hotels, shopping centers, etc. Eighty percent of their food is imported, and commodities are very expensive. The king has two wives, has divorced one and married another, but wife number one is still top wife. He has ten children with these three ladies. Women are not veiled but completely covered except face and hands. It is extremely conservative Islam, and it seems positively medieval.

This was one of the most fascinating days of our lives. We boarded our buses at 8:30 a.m. and drove directly to the "water village" called Kampong Ayer. It was actually twenty-eight villages all connected and completely built over the Brunei River. Everything—houses, mosques, stores, and schools—is all built on stilts, and access is only by water taxi. We were loaded into long boats, about twenty people per boat, and taken to this village of 30,000 people. It was pouring down rain, so there wasn't a dry square inch on any of us. The wooden steps down to the boats were treacherous, and we climbed down clutching to each other and our guides so as not to fall into the river, which runs with raw sewage. There were no handrails of any kind.

We arrived at the village (our pictures are astounding) and got off the boats to visit a longhouse. This was a Muslim family of thirty-five members who all live together; they just add more rooms as needed, which is why these are called longhouses. We had to remove our shoes before entering and went into a very large living room/reception hall with many couches and chairs. We were served hot tea in special glasses and refreshments as one would have served at a wedding. It was very lovely, and the family members were so gracious. After tea and thanking our hosts, we went back to the long boats and back to the buses. This experience was worth the whole tour. We would not have missed this for anything. Our next stop was to the Royal Regalia building where the royal jewels used in official ceremonies were kept. Also displayed was the royal chariot, which was twenty-four-carat gold, along with the collection of the sultan's gold and silver articles and treasury. Again we removed our shoes, and no pictures could be taken. Our purses and cameras were taken at the door and handed back to us when we left.

We were then taken to the crown jewel of Brunei: the Omar Ali Saifuddin Mosque with twenty-nine gold plated domes. Because the king is the twenty-ninth sultan, of course it had to have twenty-nine gold domes. It was very impressive and elegant in every possible way. Now, here is where Islam hurts. We were separated, men and women. We, of course, had head scarves. The men needed nothing but what they were wearing. They went in immediately while we ladies waited outside until our guide obtained long, black robes for us to wear. We are without shoes again, and then we were considered fit to enter. We were told that we must cover our beautiful bodies so as not to distract the men from concentrating on prayer and Allah. The mosque room of prayer was opulent and beautiful with marble, gold, crystal lighting, and magnificent rugs. It was stunning and felt very sterile.

We again found our shoes and went to our buses to go next to view the king's palace. We couldn't see much except the gates and gold domes. Jack took what pictures he could, and we went on to the next stop, the Brunei Museum, where we saw traditional weapons and antique brassware. There was an Islam gallery, but most interesting was the exhibit of oil discovery and production.

There were no hawkers here. They don't need it; their wealth was everywhere. Our young guide won our hearts at the end of the tour by saying that he is a Roman Catholic from the Philippines, and he is "tolerated." He will never have a job in the government, but if his religion is tolerated, it is a good place to live. Only 10 percent of the population represent all the other religions of the world.

Again, we were happy to see "mother" ship. Jack had our worship at 5:00 p.m. tonight, but after dinner he went to bed because of his cold. He did not feel able to have the night services for the crew today. Hope he is better tomorrow for class. It was an amazing day.

Monday, February 25

Today was a nice calm sea day. The sun actually tried to shine a bit this morning. It stayed bright but never did really clear. We are apparently in a rainy season locally. We are sailing up the coast of northern Malaysia. We will dock in the Philippine Islands tomorrow at 8:00 a.m. We are both recovering from our ship's crud. It's more than a head cold thing, with lingering coughs. Class was very interesting as Jack told about the three emotions depicted in the Psalms: glad, sad, and mad. What was particularly interesting was the reference to collecting one's tears in a tear vase during the mourning process. After class many of us came to our cabins to watch the Academy Awards that had occurred in the US last night. We had lunch, and then Jack worked on his next class material while I spent the time in the library.

As we were getting dressed for dinner, our table friend Bob called and asked that we meet him and Jacquie at the Sports Bar before dinner. We said we would be glad to and met them as agreed. When we arrived and ordered our wine, they presented us with an envelope that contained two tickets for the overland chartered flight to the Taj Mahal in India. We had not planned to go to the Taj because the cost was more than we could handle. We were not only stunned but overwhelmed by their kindness and generosity. They said that now all of us at our table will be able to see it together. Jack was speechless (rare for him), and I just wept. It was a gift of a lifetime, and we look forward with joy and anticipation to sharing this wonderful adventure with these dear people.

Tomorrow will be another beautiful day as we reach Manila. Jean, another of our table friends, will spend it in the dentist's office there. She broke a crown and needs a repair. The ship made the appointment for her and will provide a shuttle for her. Many of our crew are from the Philippines, and over a thousand of their family members are expected on board for a reunion with their family crew member. Also expected are about two hundred travel agents from Manila to tour the ship and have lunch. It will be a busy day on board while we are touring onshore. What fun!

Tuesday, February 26

Today we are in Manila in the Philippines. It was a very exciting morning. We docked at 8:00 a.m. with a wonderful Philippine band playing, with many young people playing their instruments and marching. It was so festive. Also stalls under tents were set up to have an actual bazaar on the dock. Many of our crew members had family waiting to board as we left to go to our buses. There were over a thousand family members visiting the ship. It was wonderful to see pictures of families being taken by everyone.

The people of Manila are very friendly and smiling and really love Americans. They still remember our help in Manila during World War II. This is a city that was completely destroyed, as was Warsaw, Poland. There is quite a lot of the old city left, but basically Manila is a new city. Our first stop was a beautiful park with many statues of their history and the founder of the country. The flowers were lovely with some I have never seen before, and purple bougainvillea was everywhere. Our next stop was Fort Santiago or Intramuros, meaning "within the walls" with barriers against constant attack. This was a Chinese settlement until the Spanish invaded. It was also a monument to Dr. Jose Razal a revered martyr who was devoted to peace and openly opposed Spain's zealots who attempted to overthrow the "pagan" religion. It was probably Buddhism. Spain ruled for three hundred years, and the influence is obvious in the religion (93 percent are Roman Catholic) and the architecture. Dr. Razal was a political prisoner and executed for inciting sedition. At this, the Filipino population erupted in a violent revolution. His statue, his museum, and even his marked footsteps to his execution are there.

As we got off our buses, we were treated to the music and dances of the Mardi Gras in Manila. The dancing was exquisite, with exuberance and joy that were infectious. The rhythmic beat was primitive and fun. This fort was also captured by the Japanese in WWII and the site of unimaginable torture and killings of both Filipinos and Americans. The cells and dungeons were on display, but Jack and I passed on that one as all the instruments of torture were on display as well. It was heartbreaking, and as the Japanese retreated from the city they left behind over 100,000 people killed with bayonets. Such horror and devastation are still felt here.

Our tour was of "Old Manila" and its history, so we then visited the Casa Manila, a very beautiful museum and 19th century villa—apartments, actually, of restored Victorian furnishings. It was very beautifully displayed and interesting. We then went to the Museum of the Chinese and Philippine Life. That too was well displayed and a very important part of Manila history. We went by the landmarks of Manila Cathedral and San Agustin Church, the nation's oldest churches. We then headed back to our ship by way of downtown Manila.

Throughout our tour our buses, about ten of them, were in convoy with police escorts the whole way. This is the only way we could ever get through the traffic. It is a city of seventeen million people, and I have never seen such crowds. Our port guide told us that this is just the beginning of the crowds we will encounter in other Asian cities. The driving is insane, and the roads not wide enough to handle passing very well. As a truck (semi) passed our bus, he simply drove up on the sidewalk, and the pedestrians just had to scramble. I thought some of our passengers on the bus, many type A men, were about to pass out as our driver maneuvered through it all. I just refused to look out the window at all.

As we got back to our ship, we were very late for lunch, but time becomes irrelevant on these tours, and as Jack went to lunch, I ambled through the stalls on the dock, enjoying the beautiful handwork, shells, and fabrics there. The experience of Manila is memorable, and I learned much about the city and its collaboration with us in WWII. The people are beautiful—attractive, gracious, and friendly. Getting to know our crew is wonderful because they exemplify the very best of the Philippines.

At dinner our wine steward, who is Filipino, said he was both happy and sad. He was with his family for a day but will not see them again for five months. They make hard choices. We all met at dinner except Dick and Jean. Jean had her dental work done but is not feeling well tonight. Hope she feels better tomorrow. Tomorrow is a sea day, and Jack's class resumes. We need the rest after such a busy day.

Wednesday, February 27

Wow! Today we awoke to high seas with fifteen-foot waves and were pitching and rolling all day. We had to move about cautiously and hold on to rails, furniture, and each other. Also the barf bags at the elevators were out again.

Jack and I feel we are on the mend and aren't so tired. His class was wonderful, and he gave us the historical background of the Hellenistic (Greek) culture that permeated the society in Jesus's time. We needed to know this for the lectures coming in the future. After class I went to a port lecture on Vietnam, which looks like a wonderful country to explore. We dock at Hong Kong at 7:00 a.m., and Barbara, our port lecturer, will be giving continued commentary as we enter this famous and beautiful harbor. Rolls, juice, and coffee will be served on deck as we arrive and take pictures. We are taking the walking three-hour tour of the Kowloon Mong Kok area and explore the flower street markets, the bird street, and the jade market. Sounds exotic, and we all had to have our temperatures taken on ship before we docked so that we don't carry SARS into the country. We had a quiet afternoon and then dinner with our table friends. Jacquie was ill, so she and Bob were not there. We brought our purchases from Manila to show and tell. It is always a fun time.

After dinner we went to the show and saw Jim Coston. a very talented banjo player, and Jamie Frasier, a young man from England who sang beautifully in Big Band style. Good show, and we haven't felt well enough to go before tonight. Feels good to be more active again. Tomorrow will be a fun day.

Thursday, February 28

Today, we arrived in beautiful Hong Kong. We really love Hong Kong! It is such a great and comfortable mix of the old and new worlds. Our tour started later today so we had a more leisurely breakfast and then met our buses for a walking market tour. What fun that was. We drove to the bird market, where they sold lovely caged birds of all kinds. The Chinese love birds and keep them as pets. They even walk their birds in the park, carrying them in cages. However, only the men walk the birds. Our guide didn't know why, but said it's a "guy" thing to do. The cages were so pretty and ornate that I would have loved to buy one, but I know would never be able to bring it in our luggage. That fact does limit your buying somewhat.

We then walked through the flower market and have never seen such a magnificent profusion of flowers. All cut flowers usually. The lily blooms were larger than dinner plates. The fragrance was beautiful. There is no agriculture in Hong Kong and no yards or gardens. Land is at such a premium that people all live in high-rise apartments fifty or seventy or more stories up. Consequently, people buy flowers daily because they can't grow them.

We later arrived at the jade market. Now this was a sight to behold. There were two huge buildings of bazaar type settings of nothing but jade and pearls in every conceivable image and setting. Jack and I had so much fun with our newfound talent for haggling. We got some pretty good deals, and all were happy in the process. The hawkers were persistent but not overbearing and in-your-face as they were in Bali. I understand it will become that way again in India and Istanbul.

It was only a three-hour tour, so Jack and I came back to the ship for lunch and then went out again just to experience the people and explore on our own. Next to the pier where we were docked was a fabulous upscale shopping mall. We wandered around there, bought a new Casio camera at a terrific price, and then did some other Christmas shopping as well. We took our purchases back to the ship and then got on the water taxi to go to Hong Kong Island. Actually Hong Kong is in two sections—partly on the Chinese mainland, called Kowloon, where we were docked, and then Hong Kong proper. There is a tunnel under the harbor, but most people take the water taxis, and they are great fun as you get a little tour of the coastline. We arrived on the Hong Kong side and took a double-decker open-air tram bus that took us to Victoria Mountain, where another tram conveyed us to the peak.

That was an experience; we felt we were going straight up leaning onto our backs in this tram, but when we arrived at the top, the view was spectacular, taking in all of Hong Kong, Kowloon, and the harbor's panorama.

This was where we could truly see the smog of China. People walk around with masks on all the time. Some don't, and I fear for their future health. They use coal in their industry and have no environmental guidelines in place at this time. It is just like the US in the '30s and '40s. This is a beautiful, clean city otherwise, and I have never seen so much neon lighting even at Times Square in NYC. The architecture is so new with an older structure tucked in and around it all. Skyscrapers are everywhere, and more are under construction.

On our way home we passed several Buddhist monks in their flowing saffron-colored robes, and as we got on the bus to come back to the ship, it was crammed with the cutest little Asian children, all in school uniforms. Many smiled, waved, and shouted "hello" in Chinese to us. We smiled and waved back. They were all so precious and so confident and friendly. Of course, there were many teachers with them as well.

That evening we had tickets to a local restaurant for dinner and left our ship about 7:00 p.m. Hong Kong at night is ablaze, as I could ever imagine an extremely high tech city would be. We enjoyed a good Chinese buffet dinner at a dockside club and then traveled home again to prepare for tomorrow. It was a lovely day in Hong Kong.

Friday, February 29

Today was very foggy and smoggy, so we're glad we went to the peak yesterday. However, our tour today was wonderful and we did a day in the life of Hong Kong. It was a very different day than yesterday.

We first went to the Museum of History. This is a world-class museum and one of the best museums, if not the best, that we have ever experienced. It began with Hong Kong four hundred million years ago and spanned to present day. It also depicted the cultural history, which was amazing to see.

We then went to a Taoist temple. It was fascinating in that people were everywhere burning incense sticks and buying fruit of all kinds, fans, dolls and other articles that were painted all gold and red to present to God out of their respect. In a fenced-off area, many people were kneeling in prayer with their presented goods laid out in front of them with their incense burning. It didn't seem respectful to take pictures of them in prayer, but our guide encouraged us to do so. She then took us to an area where there were rows of fortunetellers' booths. After praying, people go there for advice on decisions they must make. Astrology and zodiac signs are all calculated into the fortune. Amazing, as we are gaining so much firsthand knowledge about religions of the world. It was particularly interesting that our guide is a Taoist and was able to explain it all to us so well. However, she did speak of the fortunetellers with tongue in cheek.

We then went to a walled garden in Kowloon that was beautiful as only Asian people can create. This park was once an area where hundreds of squatters lived. The government then built huge apartment complexes for them across from the garden/park and created this beautiful space with moon gates, pebbled walks, flowers, trees, and pagodas. We ended our tour at the bird market and then went back for lunch and a restful afternoon.

After dinner I went to the Chinese cultural show at the theatre, and Jack stayed in to prepare for his class tomorrow. Tomorrow is a sea day, and then it's on to Vietnam. We are now in the northern hemisphere; we crossed the equator back in Bali and didn't even realize it.

Hi, everyone:

No, we are not lost at sea. So sorry this didn't get to you on our usual Friday, but our position to the satellite is such that we couldn't get online for a long time, and it was using up minutes, so we will hold off until we leave Singapore. Singapore is wonderful, a city we really hope to see again in our lifetime. It is vibrant, colorful, clean, beautiful, and safe and has many, many rules and laws about cleanliness and safety. We've had quite a week, and the coming weeks appear to be just as exciting and exhausting.

We will leave the dock in Singapore at 8:00 p.m. tonight and head into the Indian Ocean and on to Madras, India. We will still be in Asia but leaving the South China Sea. We are so looking forward to this next leg of the journey. This is the number three segment of the cruise, and it looks exciting. About a hundred of our passengers left us, and a similar number joined us in Singapore.

We miss all of you. Stay warm, healthy, and happy, and please pray for us as we are praying for all of you.

Our love to all.

Joyce and Jack

JOURNAL # 9

Saturday, March 1

We can't believe March is here already, and two months have passed on this phenomenal cruise. Today is a sea day. We're still in the South China Sea, and the sailing is very calm. We dock in Halong Bay at Hanoi, Vietnam. This is a UNESCO World Heritage Site, and we're anxious to finally see it.

Today was a busy day. In Jack's class, he explained the history and culture around Nathaniel's statement regarding Jesus in John 1:46 (NRSV): "Can anything good come out of Nazareth?" It was fascinating, and the class continues to grow. Today was moving day for us as we moved to a different cabin because people who came on at Hong Kong paid for an outside cabin, and ours was the only one available, so now we are in an inside cabin. Very nice; more closet space, just no window. We'll have to go on deck to see what the weather is outside.

We were all at dinner tonight and just enjoyed each other's company. Jack and I went to the show to see Penny Mathisen, a young lady with a beautiful operatic voice. She sang from opera to Broadway. She was excellent, and we loved it. We look forward to another good day tomorrow.

Sunday, March 2

Today we docked in the harbor of Halong Bay near Hanoi, Vietnam. This is one of the most scenic and exotic looking harbors we've seen. There are huge limestone islands throughout the bay. *Halong* means "descending dragon." The legend says that a fierce dragon once terrorized villagers here, and a brave warrior set out to slay him. The dragon scurried out to the sea, and the people believe that like the Loch Ness Monster, "Tarasque," the dragon, is in the bay. Indeed, it is what a dragon's tail would look like with the limestone islands jutting out of the water. There are over 1,000 of them and they are quite beautiful. There are many, many caves within these rocks with some very huge ones. There were boat tours offered of the bay and caves, but they were sold out before we got on the ship. So Jack and I stayed on board and took lots of great pictures from the decks.

Jack prepared for today's 5:00 p.m. service, and it was well attended. Jean and Dick, our table friends, treated all of us to a delicious dinner at the Pinnacle Grill on board to celebrate the halfway mark of our cruise together. Jack is on his way for the 10:00 and 11:00 p.m. services for the crew. He loves doing that.

Tomorrow we dock at Da Nang, and we'll be doing a tour there. All these names are so familiar to us because we lived through the Vietnam War. Surprisingly, we learned that Vietnam is the number one vacation destination in the world today, and there is much construction of hotels, restaurants, and condo complexes everywhere. We are looking forward to tomorrow's adventure in Da Nang.

Monday, March 3

Today we docked at Da Nang, Vietnam. We boarded buses for our tour and drove about an hour through the countryside to reach the ancient city of Hoi An. This is a preserved historical center and another UNESCO World Heritage Site. In the sixteenth century it was a powerful commercial center of trade. Chinese, Japanese, and Western merchants gathered at this port for trading. Our guide took us to an "ancient" house, which was a preserved historic Chinese merchant's home—very ornate, with beautifully restored furniture.

We then were taken to a handicraft factory where we were fascinated to see rows and rows of very young girls embroidering magnificent scenes, flowers, and religious images on fabrics. These girls would hold a picture in front of them and then just embroider the same picture on cloth. No guidelines to follow at all; just freehand, so to speak. We went into a loom room where there were large basket trays of silkworms on fresh leaves, and they were creating silk pods. The girls would take these pods and place them in boiling water; when they took the pods out of the water, they gently unraveled a fine, fine thread of silk from the pod. They would then spindle it and get it ready for the large looms, where women then wove the silk cloth. There were also many trays of tiny silkworm babies growing to make silk someday. It was one of the most fascinating things we have ever seen. Many women and girls sat at tables embroidering tablecloths, bureau scarves, napkins, etc.—all for sale, of course, and very reasonable. Some people on our ship came on this particular cruise just for this stop in Vietnam and the handicraft factory. They purchased vast amounts of these beautiful products. One room was only for the clothing made of silk—beautiful items, and I had a lovely red silk jacket made. They measured me in seven minutes flat, made the jacket, and delivered it to our ship at 4:30 this afternoon. It fits perfectly. I will wear it at the formal dinner and our table picture tomorrow night.

We then spent about one and a half hours shopping at Hoi An. It was a delight browsing up and down these very simple open-air shops with all the vibrant colored wares for sale. It was amazingly cheap, and I bought two lovely lace fans, two beaded purses, and a necklace, all for $16. I'm afraid I may need to buy another suitcase just for the things we've bought thus far, and we have two more months to go. We have fabulous pictures of this very special place and the beautiful, gentle, soft-spoken people. We saw some of the devastation of the war—American bunkers. We also saw China Beach where our service people came for R & R. Very pretty area.

As we drove through the countryside, one could see very much poverty here. Our cute little guide told us she made less than $700 a month as a teacher and a part-time tour guide. Everything for them is very expensive in Vietnam, as much of their needs must be imported. Education is not free, and they can only have two children. This is a communist country, and the government is now encouraging capitalistic endeavors. Sure hope it helps the people. There were many hawkers, but they weren't obnoxious.

We had dinner with Lona and Gary, another of our table friends. The other two couples hadn't yet returned from touring. We then went back to our cabin because touring in a strange country is exhausting. I really think the extreme strangeness of such a foreign atmosphere is what exhausts us so. We went to bed early and look forward to another restful sea day tomorrow.

Tuesday, March 4

Seas were very choppy today, but not too bad for our seasick friends. Jack's class was particularly interesting because he talked about the genealogy of Jesus and the non-Jewish women mentioned in his lineage and why women were hardly mentioned at all in the male-dominated society of Jesus's times. This is so amazing to us in the twenty-first century.

I attended a port lecture on Singapore, and we will have two days to be in that great port city. There is so much history and beauty there to see and learn. I also went to the lecture by the speaker Kate Ross on the Khmer Empire and Angkor Wat in Cambodia. It was very well done, and I learned much about that part of the world. Our tour tomorrow doesn't take us there, but many are going on a three-day overland tour into that area of Asia. We rested after lunch and read and worked on the computer.

Before dinner we learned that Jean and Dick, our table friends, had received news that Dick's sister died today. Our table friends wanted to support them as much as we could, so Jack is going to have a memorial service for Dick's sister on our next sea day, which is Thursday. It's a vivid realization that life goes on outside as well as inside our cocoon world here on MS *Amsterdam*. In two months we have become "family," sharing our lives very closely. It is very good.

Wednesday, March 5

Wow! We are in the port of Phu My, Vietnam, and has this ever been a day of many emotions—some of such intensity that some of our passengers couldn't even go ashore because of their memories of being here during the war in the '70s. However, we did go on tour today after some problems getting off without a shore pass in lieu of carrying our passports. HAL told us that as crew members we didn't need shore passes, because we were on a list. Well, someone must have lost the list because as we tried to go ashore and pass through the checkpoint, no way the immigration officers would hear of it. "No passes, no passes," they kept saying. We explained several times, and finally a ship's representative went with us and they let us through with many smiles and apologies. That was the first day, and our bus had to wait for us to get through.

The second day Jack went to the gangway early to watch how immigration was handling our shore passes and saw that it would be easy to just slip around the crowd as immigration was stamping others' shore passes—which is what we did. Now, I'm one who stammers and feels guilty when at the Canadian border I'm asked where I was born, so all day I kept wondering if we were going to be clapped in irons and hauled to a communist prison, never to be seen again. Finally we boarded our buses and drove one and a half hours to Ho Chi Minh City (Saigon). We passed cows wandering along the roadside, rice paddies, and many water buffalo. They must use work animals because modern machinery would not work in a rice paddy full of water. It is a very primitive method of farming.

Unfortunately, Vietnam is not a very clean country, and trash is everywhere. We saw people just tossing bottles and paper along the streets. There are very few cars because they must be imported, and the very low income levels (average income is thirty cents per hour) as well as extremely high taxes on the vehicles mean the average person cannot afford a car. Hence, motor scooters and bicycles are everywhere with masses of them along the road with no regard to lanes and going in and out and between cars, buses, and trucks. It's a wild scene.

Our young Vietnamese guide was a delight. He was extremely well educated and very personable, with a great sense of humor, and told really good jokes along with his presentation. This young man will own the tour company one day. Our first stop was to a shopping area with fairly good facilities (no toilet paper). He called it a ladies' "happy room," but men can just use a "happy tree." Indeed, Jack saw at least twelve or fifteen men in the city using "happy trees." At our happy room stop there were many hawkers. It must be a popular tourist bus stop. Also, we saw several beggars who were quite horribly maimed with limbs missing and exposed bodies so burns would show. Some were older and probably injured in the war or burned as young children. It was heart-wrenching but a reality here.

We had about an hour's drive into Saigon, and our guide told us about the agriculture of Vietnam as we were passing fertile farmland. Vietnam is the second largest exporter of coffee in the world, after only Brazil. He told us something that was hard for us to believe but assured us it is absolutely true. The area of Vietnam highlands where the best coffee grows has a little weasel-like animal that loves the coffee "cherries." In each cherry there are two coffee beans. This little weasel eats these coffee cherries but can only digest the flesh and outer shell of the cherries; the bean itself is indigestible, so out it comes. Then it is gathered, cleaned (one hopes), and sold as the most expensive and most delicious of all the coffees. The Vietnamese people actually call this "Weasel [you know what] Coffee." After about ten minutes of howling laughter, he told us that the coffee beans absorb some of the enzymes of the weasel's intestine making it the most delicious and preferred coffee in the country. This is a country that also delights in eating snake meat. Ugh!

Our next stop was a zoo with a botanical garden and park. It was very beautiful with topiaries and Buddhist shrines. Some 85 percent of the people are Buddhist, another 10 percent are Roman Catholic and Protestant, and the last 5 percent are Muslim or Hindu. The Buddhists generally have a very gentle soul, and our guide explained that there's no road rage here other than foreigners because Buddhists believe that rage comes back to you. We stopped next at the Notre Dame Cathedral but were unable to go inside, as it was closed. We also went into the post office, which was a lovely building built by the French during their occupation.

We were then treated to a magnificent buffet lunch at the Hotel Equatorial in Saigon. It served all Vietnamese food, and it was delicious. The five-star hotel itself was gorgeous, with a casino and many amenities not even seen in the US. The young women at the reception desk were lovely in traditional dresses that wedding attendants would wear. Of course, they were all in red because red in Asia means good luck. Their headpieces were beautiful, and one young lady allowed us to take her picture as she explained about her attire.

After this delicious lunch, we boarded our buses after passing through the hordes of hawkers that followed us from stop to stop.

They must have done very well with us because many bought from them. They were quite charming, especially a little girl about ten years old and her brother, about fifteen, with their beautiful smiles and many expressions of thank-you. The people are gentle and sweet-natured with oriental grace. We then drove past the former site of the American Embassy and the scene of the memorable helicopter airlift of people as the US left Vietnam. Madeline Albright came here and ordered it to be torn down because of the horrible memories it harbored, and now the American Consulate stands in its place. No pictures were allowed here, and the guards saw to it as well.

We then went to the Reunification Hall where at the end of the war, a Russian and Chinese tank crashed through the front gates. The South Vietnamese president surrendered to the North Vietnamese in the cabinet room just inside the entrance hall. We were then taken to the basement and to the war room with all the strategic communication systems, maps, and lists of US troops and allies all still in place, and even the maps of caves and tunnel routes where the Vietcong gained supplies. Three million Vietnamese people were killed in the war. It was a dismal site, and emotions were at the surface for all of us because it happened not very long ago, and most of us couldn't believe we were standing in Saigon today. My thoughts went back to the beautiful and moving Vietnam memorial in Washington, DC, and all that we lost as well.

Our next stop was to the Ho Chi Minh City Museum. It was a museum of religious culture with many happy Buddhas around and many photos of the city at different times in history. It was not a museum that was well displayed; it was even quite dusty. The people are poor, and it is not funded well. The Communists maintain only what they deem important, and this obviously wasn't to them. But the building itself was lovely, as French architecture can be. It was the home of the first French governor of Vietnam back in the 1800s.

We boarded our buses very tired, emotionally wrung out, and ready to retreat back, shamefully, to our luxury again. There is such inequity in this world. We had dinner and now a good night's sleep. It will be a good restful sea day tomorrow. We sure need it.

Thursday, March 6

It is a good sea day, with calm seas. After a restful night's sleep, Jack's class was great with many comments and observations. I went to a very interesting lecture by Ruth Turton all about tea. It is a four-part series, and this one was "Totally Tea" about the history of tea, the growing and identification of tea, and blends. I look forward to the other lectures. I learned quite a lot about teas and proper brewing methods. We have teas on ship most afternoons. I've never attended but will try one soon.

We had a lunch date with a couple from our class, and they are delightful company. They lived in Spain and China for many years, as the gentleman worked with Phillips 66 Oil Company. Hope we can meet again and get better acquainted. There are so many wonderful people here, and we never tire of meeting new ones. We had a restful afternoon working on the computer, napping, and reliving yesterday's adventure. It takes a while to process such emotion.

At 5:00 p.m. and before dinner, our table friends had a memorial service for Dick's sister. Dick and Jean are our table friends as well. Jack helped Dick and Jean understand their grieving process, and it was wonderful that we all could support them in this way. Guilt is a big factor when you can't get back for the funeral of a loved one. Hopefully, this will help them. We came back to our cabins after dinner and tried to go on line to receive our email, but the system was really slow tonight, and it would waste our minutes waiting. So we signed off and will try again tomorrow when we dock in Singapore. We are looking forward to our adventures in Singapore for the next two days.

Hi, everyone:

Here is our next journal. It is always exciting and very interesting.

Love to all,

Joyce and Jack

JOURNAL # 10

Friday, March 7

Today, we are in the beautiful harbor of Singapore. The symbol is a merlion, a lion's head with a fish's tail. *Singa* means lion, and we saw this symbol all over the city. We awoke later today because we had our tour at 2:15 p.m. So I ate a late breakfast (Jack ate earlier), and then we just chatted in the Lido for a bit. Had lunch with our really nice Jewish friends from our class and then went to the lounge to get ready to board our buses for a panoramic tour of Singapore.

It is a spotlessly clean city with laws and rules and signs everywhere. Jaywalkers are fined on the spot. There's no littering, smoking, or gum chewing, which carry huge fines. Drug traffickers are sentenced to death by hanging. One can never carry a gun, which is also a hanging offense. Scary! Everywhere you hear that it is an absolutely safe place, day or night. It is the wealthiest city in Asia, and it shows. Three things make them so: the container port (the largest in Asia), the financial district, and tourism. Ten percent is reclaimed land, and it is at a premium, so they build upward. As a result, there are many beautiful skyscrapers everywhere. Three million people are in Singapore, and it too is a crowded Asian city and lovely in all respects. There is no smog at all. The people are beautiful, helpful, and friendly.

We boarded our buses for a good mile walk through a wonderful terminal mall for shopping. We drove through the

Arab Street seeing beautiful mosques. Then we drove through Little India where there were Hindu temples. We continued to drive through a huge Chinatown. Most people here are Chinese, and Chinatown is its largest district. Singapore is divided into four districts really. The architecture is being preserved there, and they are unable to change anything outside the buildings, so there were gorgeous carved friezes, roofs, and windows.

We then went to a WWI and WWII monument to take pictures in the colonial district where all their many historic buildings were located. From here we went on to a wonderfully ornate Taoist temple and the Singapore people are about 60 percent Buddhist or Taoist. The remainder are Christian, Muslim, and Hindu. Our last stop was a gemstone and metal (gold, silver, etc.) jewelry handicraft factory where we could watch them cut the beautiful gems. Of course, much was for sale, and Jack bought a lovely watch, and I got one free: buy one, get one free deal. Great, and Singapore dollars are 40 percent less than US dollars, and so it was a great price.

We came back to the ship by way of Orchard Road, which is a very exclusive and magnificent shopping district. Every store in the world is represented here, and there were thousands. It was a shopper's paradise. Instead of going back to the ship for dinner, our friends Jacquie and Bob invited us to dine with them and found a wonderful Japanese restaurant with a grille in the middle of the table where the food is served to you raw, and you cook it in your own little grille. It was not only fun but delicious. We staggered back home to our cabins, very tired, to get ready for another day tomorrow in Singapore. This is one of those cities you really hope you can visit again.

Saturday, March 8

Today is beautiful. Sunny, hot, not too humid, and Singapore is so clear and clean. We arose early and went out on our own for the morning. A wonderful cable car traveled over the Singapore River and right over our ship to the island of Santosa, a lush rain forest island and very lovely. Just for fun, we got round trip tickets to ride across and back again in about thirty minutes, and the view of the harbor and city was spectacular. We were fortunate that we were alone in our car so Jack could move around and get lots of great pictures.

We then came back to the cruise terminal center and walked around this huge complex and did a bit of shopping. It was fun and leisurely. It was complicated getting on and off the ship because we had to constantly stand in long lines for customs and passport checks. We had a good lunch with a retired doctor of internal medicine from Florida whose wife was on an overland trip for three days to Angkor Wat, Cambodia. He remained on board because he has macular degeneration and felt safer here.

We then went through immigration for the third time today to board our buses for the Mysteries of the Orient tour. It was all about the concept, thousands of years old, of feng shui. This was about the five elements of life—fire, water, wood, metal, and earth—and how in Singapore when the city began building all of these magnificent structures, three masters of feng shui were consulted regarding the placement of the buildings, their sizes in relationship to each other, their proximity to water, and the building materials used, as well as colors of the buildings. Every fountain in Singapore sprays inward rather than outward because water flowing represents money or prosperity, and you always want it to come in, not out. Right? Even the colors of logos, interiors, and some exteriors are important. The color red not only is for luck (luck is a big factor in Asian culture) but for authority. Blue is for wealth. So there is not a bank in Singapore or China in which red and blue does not predominate. The architecture is beautiful, and the buildings have no sharp corners but are angled, rounded, or inverted. Ying and Yang are prominent in structures.

It's about the flow of energy, positive or negative, and certainly negative energy is to be avoided.

We first went to a beautiful shopping mall—a very successful, crowded one with the world's largest fountain in the center with water flowing inward, again synonymous with prosperity. Then to the famous financial district, and it is no accident that it is immediately on the Singapore River. The structures flow so beautifully with harmony. Now I know why the buildings here and in Hong Kong strike me as so pleasing to see and so harmonious. We also went into Chinatown to see some very old historic buildings that reflect the same concept. Of course, there are some buildings not built on that concept, but strangely enough, people know that, and so they are relatively suspicious and so will not buy office or store space in these buildings.

In Chinatown we went to a shop where a Chinese gentleman painted each of our names on red fans with Chinese characters. They are beautiful, and we got each of our grandson's names written for them in Chinese. They will be great to frame for them. Our guide then took us to the headquarters of feng shui in a commercial area near the Night Market in Chinatown to show us the consultation rooms, etc. Our guide had studied with this famous master in Singapore. We loved hearing about the city planning on this concept, but the personal determination of making decisions regarding your birthday year and time in consultation we took with a grain of salt. It reminded us of astrology here in the US. However, it was very interesting to know that this concept is alive and well in Singapore.

We came back "home" too late to have dinner at our table so we just got a quick supper at the Lido and then went back to our cabin and to bed. Ipi, our cabin steward, showed me how to make towel animals. Every night we have the cutest animals on our bed made from our towels. He showed me how to make a monkey and a dog. Can't wait to show little grandsons Jack and Alex. We set our clocks back an hour tonight. Church tomorrow and a sea day. Ah! Restful.

Today was our sixty-fifth day at sea. We have forty-nine days to go, but none of us wants to count or think about it. We have traveled by sea, as of Singapore, 19,853 miles. It is a beautiful hot, sunny sea day, about 80 degrees F. We had a lifeboat drill this morning for everyone, a refresher for us oldies and to orient the new people who came on in Singapore. That was the beginning of our third leg of this journey going into India. We are now sailing in the Straits of Malacca with Sumatra on our port side (left) and Malaysia on our starboard (right) as we leave Indonesia, China, and the Spice Islands. We are heading into the Bay of Bengal to Chennai (Madras, the British name). The cities of India are now reverting back to their ancient names before British settlement came and changed them. It's confusing.

We had worship today at 9:00 a.m., and Jack's sermon was about the temptations of Christ in the wilderness in relation to the temptations we face as we grow older. Every seat was filled in the service and the theatre holds about 150 people.

After lunch I went to a port lecture about Chennai and surrounding cities. Tomorrow Jack and I will choose and schedule our tours for this part of the journey. That is always fun, and we'll have some great ones to choose from, including Istanbul and Egypt on this part. I was finally able to get online, now that we have left Singapore and our satellite position has changed, and I was able to get email notes and send out journal # 9 to everyone, a day or two late for that reason. Dinner was a Singapore theme night with all decorations (flags) and food of the area. Delicious! We all wore the beautiful mandarin outfits we bought in Asia. Jack got his lovely blue and gold one in Singapore, and I got my red and gold one in Hoi An, Vietnam. After dinner we saw the movie *Juno*. It was a very good movie, and Jack is now at his 10:00 and 11:00 p.m. services for the crew.

Tomorrow is another sea day and more to do and learn and, of course, rest. I love these sea days.

Monday, March 10

Today is rainy and cloudy, but it cleared midday to merely overcast and humid. Jack's class was fascinating as he explained the whole system of ancient sacrifice. We chose and scheduled our tours for this part of our voyage, and it looks really exciting and truly exotic. The Taj Mahal is part of it, and we fly there from the ship at 3:30 a.m. on March 17. It'll be exhausting but unbelievable to be there. We can sleep the next day.

I attended the lecture on tea again today and discovered how to make regular tea decaffeinated. Very simple: Put the tea bags in a teapot, and pour boiling water over them. Let it stand for no more than forty-five seconds. Remove the tea bags, pour out the water, and then pour boiling water over the tea bags again, and brew as usual. Amazing! Decaffeinated tea. Also learned that the tea plant is a camellia variety and that herb teas are not teas at all but *tisanes* —infusions of herb leaves. Good and interesting lecture.

We received a call from the front office today to bring our immunization records to determine if we have had our yellow fever shots. It seems the passengers do not need yellow fever shots, but the Indian Department of Health is demanding that all of us who are service staff (thirteen of us) do, and the ship won't be cleared to dock until we do. We went to the medical clinic to get our shots, only to learn that they do not have the shots to give us on board, but India will let them know prior to docking whether the ship's administration will take us somewhere to get them or will come aboard to give them to us. It would have been so easy to have gotten them when we received all our other ones before we left home. We discovered India really likes to confuse cruise ships—and all other tourists for that matter. It is very frustrating for the HAL administration but typical behavior for India, we understand. We just have to wait for them to notify us.

Since tonight is a formal night, all of us at our table met at the professional photographer's for a picture of our group. We all looked wonderful in our formal attire, and it will be great to have this photo of such terrific friends. After dinner Jack and I went to the performance of Ian Cooper, a very skillful and talented violinist. He played from classical to hoedown, and it was great fun.

There will be another good sea day tomorrow and then Chennai, India. How exciting. We put our clocks back a half hour tonight to be in sync with India. That's strange. I'm sure we'll catch up with the other half hour somewhere along the way.

Tuesday, March 11

Today is another beautiful hot sea day. Jack's class was very good today, and we have several new members who came on in Singapore. Jack explained all about Passover, the Last Supper, and the sacrificial lamb's slaughter in the temple. It was spellbinding to know that the Hebrews were celebrating Passover, a festival of freedom of bondage in Egypt, while in Jerusalem under the thumb of Rome. It's no wonder Rome had a hair trigger at that time. On this world cruise it is customary to have Passover with a Seder meal scheduled for April 19, and we Christians are invited. What a great experience for us, and we hear the ship does it beautifully along with a dinner after. It will be held in the Lido with two settings, feeding about 200 to 300 people. I'm sure our class will be there in full, especially after Jack's lectures about it.

After my exercising session, we had lunch with Rabbi Bob and Sheila, comparing notes on our experiences and those of some of our passengers. It seems we're a support group of four. Actually, we're all flying by the seat of our pants because this is their first world cruise as well, and they too, had less than a month notice as the usual rabbi's wife was very ill, and they couldn't come.

After lunch we checked our email. It's so great to hear from home friends and family. Then we did some special laundry. As much as I love the laundry service, they insist on ironing all our knit shirts, and that makes them huge. So had to rewash some and hope they would shrink in a hot dryer. Most did, thank goodness. After dinner we just strolled around this magnificent ship and talked with folks we knew. Getting to know more people each day. It's wonderful.

We're getting ready for our big day tomorrow docking in Chennai. I checked with the medical clinic today about further word on our yellow fever shots, and the nurse said that since we're over sixty, we shouldn't have them, as the risk of complications is greater than the risk of contracting the disease. We'll see tomorrow if we can get off the ship scot-free. Also India's Health Department is ignoring emails from the ship's administration, and the administration is confused about the whole situation. It'll be interesting to see what happens. However, Jack and I are all packed up and ready to go out at 9:15 a.m. tomorrow on a Discover Chennai tour. It'll be exciting, and we can't wait to see India, even though I know we will see things we wish we hadn't. But this is our world, and we are determined to dive right into it—and pray.

Wednesday, March 12

We are in India—*wow!* Our most exotic port, with seven and a half million people—mass humanity. Are we going to be able to get off the ship without our yellow fever shots? And we had no shore passes at our door as promised. Still, we actually did get off, much to our amazement. Not one word was mentioned about our shots, so we're thinking India decided to forget the whole thing including our shore passes. It has been mass confusion. Thirteen of us are supplemental staff, neither passengers nor crew. We're passengers when it's convenient or crew when it's convenient (so we're told). They call us the "funny people," and it is fun learning about the subtleties of a luxury cruise liner. As in any industry, it would make you wonder. Because of the fiasco, no one got on their tours in time, and our shore passes were finally found after an hour of searching.

We too actually were able to board our bus. The buses were comfortable and clean but with rumpled carpeting, which tripped everyone. The microphone was broken so our dear lady guide, who was very smart, personable, and lovely in a beautiful sari, had to shout in her thick Indian accent with a lisp. It was one of our many challenges today. However, she was really sweet and repeated everything for us at the front of the bus and again for those in the back. As we left the dock, we saw several elderly ladies scraping some black mud off the road around the dock. We learned it was coal dust for them to use for cooking and heating; they were gleaners.

As we traveled in incredible traffic with absolutely no regard for lanes or right or left sides of the road, we saw tuk-tuks, which are three-wheel vehicles. These are really cute golf cart–type vehicles and take tourists everywhere. Saw some very ancient rickshaws as well. Motor scooters, bikes, trucks, buses, and cars were everywhere. It was astounding. We drove by fishing villages on an enormous beach area where actual tents and huts and just tarps thrown over sticks were where people lived. Fishing boats, nets, and laundry all were lying on the beach drying. It was so ancient and primitive looking.

We drove directly into downtown to the Hindu Kapaleeshwarar Temple. The bus parked right in the middle of a downtown street with traffic congested beyond belief so we could disembark. We walked a long way down a market street looking exactly as it has for thousands of years, with women in gorgeous saris and men in madras plaid loincloths that could be let down as long wraparound skirts. The men had various headdresses, but none of the women did unless they were Muslim. Didn't see many.

At the temple there was a huge pool with running water for the people to bathe and wash themselves before going into the temple for prayer. Jack and I looked in the pool to see the fish and to our horror they were not fish at all but many, many eels. It made my skin crawl to think people got into this, and it didn't look any too clean to begin with.

We took many pictures of the temple but didn't go in. With no shoes allowed, we knew we would have to just throw our socks away if we did. We didn't dare take off our socks as the temple was full of mud. We were here the first day of a ten-day religious festival, and everyone was in their finery. As we left the temple area, we ran into a great religious procession with drums, traditional music, and statues being carried through the streets.

It was a miracle we found our bus. Most of us boarded, but one couple was missing, so our guide and escort had to go out looking for them in this crush of humanity. One half hour later they returned with the lady who had no idea where her husband was as they got lost and then separated by the crowds. They went out again searching and came back with another lost lady from another bus, but not the first man. They cell phoned all the other buses and found him picked up by another tour bus. Whew! All accounted for. Then we waited another half hour for some men to raise a ceremonial canopy over the road for the procession to follow under later in the day. Our dear little guide just smiled her dazzling smile and said, "Welcome to India."

We then proceeded to San Thome (St. Thomas, Jesus's disciple) Basilica. The legend is (and Jack and I really like it) that Jesus's disciple, Thomas, came to India after the crucifixion and resided here in India for twenty years. He would go to the nearby beach on the Bay of Bengal and preach the gospel, making many converts to Christianity. The Hindu fathers did not like this and murdered him. His tomb is in the beautiful Roman Catholic church along with a relic of his hand bone. Who knows? But it's a nice legend, and here is where St. Thomas is remembered.

When we arrived at the Basilica, all forty of us made a beeline for the bathrooms. I looked at the nice porcelain hole in the floor and thought, *Oh dear. With my hip replacements, how do I handle this challenge?* Ladies in Asia just squat. It's very efficient and Asian women rarely have hip problems because of this behavior. I noticed there was a faucet near the floor used for washing. Again, no toilet paper in sight. I routinely stuff my pockets with Kleenex before leaving the ship in the mornings. Nearby was a large cup used to throw water down the toilet to clean it. So, yes, just like at the doctor's office, I used the cup. It worked great, and I just washed it out thoroughly and breathed a sigh of relief. I'm going to have to carry something like that for our next tour. I may not be so lucky next time. Speaking of this lovely subject of toilets in Asia, right outside the Temple area was a sign on the back of a truck saying "Ladies Toilet," and yes, right in front of it was a hole that looked like the work of a post-hole digger. Indeed, right out in the open with everyone milling around was the ladies' toilet. Men don't bother with such niceties; just go, anyplace at any time. Except in the temple, of course.

We then went to the Government Museum to see the Bronze Gallery. It was beautifully done. Mostly of Hindu gods, Shiva and his wife from the tenth, eleventh, and twelfth centuries. By this time we were all ready for an escape hatch. Collectively, our tolerance for strangeness is very short. What was supposed to be a four-hour tour became six. No lunch, oppressive heat, and unbelievable crowds, but still I would not have missed this for anything in this world. India is horrible, yet fabulous. It is such a mixture of sounds, sights, smells, and emotions, and there was a feast of all. What a day in our memories, with Mumbai (Bombay) ahead in just three days.

We arrived, breathlessly, back at ship fifteen minutes before my pedicure appointment—to find that my operator was ill, and I had to reschedule anyway. Never sweat anything in India. You just go with the flow. It was terrific to all meet again for dinner and share our day. None of us were together on tours, so we talked forever and had to be chased out for the next dinner sitting. We were too tired and wired to do anything else but seek sanctuary in our cabins. Our first day in India: Incredible!

Thursday, March 13

Today is a sea day. Sunny in the morning, but then cloudy all day, with rain. At 8:00 a.m. I went to my rescheduled pedicure appointment and missed most of Jack's class. He said it went well.

Today there was, sadly, a "bright star" announcement into our rooms. That means someone has died on board. It was one of our wheelchair passengers. That is the third death we've had so far on ship. It really isn't surprising, especially since the average age is seventy-five. How wonderful that he died doing something he loved: cruising around the world. I understand he was on one of the tours yesterday.

After class we checked our emails and then went to lunch, where we visited with two really nice couples. One was from Portland, Oregon, and the other from Ontario. Another of our multiple world cruise sailors. It boggles our minds.

This afternoon, Jack worked on putting our two thousand pictures and more, so far, onto an external hard drive we bought in Singapore. We felt we had to back them all up just in case. Never know with computers, and these pictures are priceless to us. We may never come this way again; we hope so, but maybe we won't be invited. However, Kate Ross, one of the lecturers on board for the Exploration Series on India, is attending Jack's class and is encouraging him to be one of the Exploration lecturers on the Mediterranean cruises of his Windows of the Biblical World series. It would mean that they would fly us from ship to ship for a week or so per ship, and that doesn't sound very attractive to either of us, with all the packing and unpacking, etc. Plus, that's not really what Jack's ministry here is all about. He wants to be a spiritual leader not only a lecturer. But we know we must be open to every ministry opportunity, wherever it takes us. I worked on the journal, read, and rested. It was a good afternoon. Dinner was great and fun as usual. After dinner we attended a good movie called *The Golden Compass*—a fantasy. Back to bed and another sea day tomorrow.

We wish a very happy Easter to all of you.

This week was one of the best of our world cruise as you can tell from my descriptions of the Taj Mahal adventure. Our ship family is really a good community of wonderful folks, and we are enjoying so many of them at meals, tours together, classes, services, and lectures as well as just visiting on deck and around the ship. Our Easter sunrise service will be 6:30 a.m. out on top deck on Easter Sunday with a special brunch in the dining room at 10 a.m. It should be a spectacular worship experience on the Red Sea as we approach Egypt. We have about six days at sea before we reach Alexandria, Egypt, and our fourteen-hour tour of the pyramids in Giza. It is incredible!

Our love to each of you on this Easter 2008.

Joyce and Jack

JOURNAL # 11

Friday, March 14

A lovely warm, sunny day today at sea. Jack talked about the political and economic situation in Jerusalem, Palm Sunday, and Jesus's cursing of the fig tree, which symbolized Hebrew security: "That every man may sit under his own vine and fig tree" (Micah 4:4 NRSV). To learn of the stranglehold Rome had on the common people financially was really interesting, with more to learn tomorrow. The class continues to grow, with several of our Jewish passengers coming now as well.

After class I went to a port lecture on Salalah, Oman, our port of call after India. It's hard to think about anything beyond the Taj Mahal on the seventeenth of March, as it is such a highlight for all of us. Several have told us that the whole world tour is worth just the Taj. It's magical, and to think it is a tomb to honor an emperor's beloved wife. However, we learned a lot about Oman and look forward to that too. Jack joined me after that lecture for Kate Ross's lecture on the Taj Mahal. It was wonderful and a really good background for our trip there.

After lunch we attempted to get online but the connection was slow in the internet café, even with the tech expert helping us. Finally, we remembered our friend, Jacquie, telling us that her connection was good this morning on deck seven and inviting us to try there as well. Wow! It was a beautiful connection. We were able to receive emails and answer them in no time at all. It was great.

Dinner was formal tonight, followed by a special Bollywood awards presentation. Bollywood is one of the film industries in India. Many movies are made in India. We didn't stay long and headed up to our cabin and a good book and bed. We sure are old homebodies. Look forward to a good day tomorrow.

Saturday, March 15 – The Ides of March

Today was cloudy and warm. Calm seas, and we're now in the Arabian Sea; love all these exotic names that I've only read about in my lifetime. Tomorrow we dock at 6:00 a.m. at Mumbai (Bombay), India. Today, Jack talked about the temple, which was the financial institution for the Hebrews. Also we learned about Jesus turning over the money changers' tables; it was at this point that the authorities decided to kill him. We now have more Jewish couples in our class, and they keep saying, "We've never learned this stuff." They feel comfortable with us because Jack is teaching only first-century history and culture and our joint Jewish and Christian heritage. He is not going into any church doctrine because we have a complete spectrum of faiths represented. It is absolutely wonderful, and we see it building great community on ship because we are concentrating on our commonality and not our differences.

After class I went to our last tea lecture and then lunch with two new ladies on board from Princeton, New Jersey. They were a delight, and we hope to meet with them again for lunch. This afternoon we checked our emails and answered some, changed some US currency into rupees as we can do on board, and checked on our shore passes. It seems again we are "crew" and don't have to go through immigration proceedings as the passengers do. We're meeting the craft couple, Doug and Gretchen, to tour around on our own tomorrow morning. They have been here seven times and know the ropes; they have been gracious enough to go with us. We're looking forward to seeing Gandhi's House and Museum and the laundry. These are "not to miss sites" in Mumbai.

Had dinner with our dear table friends, and then saw the show afterwards. It was a good British comedian. Love British humor, and he was very funny. We are now sailing north along the coast of western India and are excited to see Mumbai in the morning.

Sunday, March 16

Ah, India! Mumbai—or Bombay, meaning "good bay"—is incredible. After getting our shore passes easily this time, we met Gretchen and Doug to tour this wonderful city together. We hired a taxi and a good English-speaking driver for only $25 each for five hours. Excellent price.

Our first stop was the magnificent Victoria Terminus or train station. It is the most ornate and beautiful of any Victorian building in the world. The British built it in the 1880s, and it honors the queen's golden jubilee. We went inside where the trains came in. Eleven million people a day come in and out of this station. It is mind boggling. People were all over that train and even hanging on to the sides as it came into the slip inside the station. We took pictures of people with everything imaginable on their heads and inside the coaches, which were filthy and little more than cattle cars. People were sleeping everywhere on the ground, and we learned that people come into the city to rent a sleeping spot on the sidewalks and alleys because it is guarded and safe there. Many women were carrying infants and begging. We learned from our guide to never give them anything as they rent these babies just for the purpose of begging. We also saw small street children seven or eight years old sleeping soundly on sidewalks with people walking around and over them. It was heart-wrenching to see their malnutrition. We were also warned never to give the children anything, because then more than a hundred may stampede you, all begging at once, and this can be dangerous. They are also good at picking your pockets. So sad. However, never did we feel frightened or threatened in any way even in the most crowded situations.

Our driver then took us to a Jain temple. This is the most conservative of all Hindu faiths; they never kill anything and even wear masks so as not to breathe in bugs or gnats and harm them. These people do not cremate or bury the dead but hang them in trees, greatly sheltered where you never see them, and let the vultures clean the bones. They then bury the bones. We went into the beautiful hanging gardens in Bombay and saw these "Towers of Silence" where this is done. We also saw hundreds of vultures circling so we knew they were feeding. We, of course, never saw the dead. A grizzly thought, but quite efficient when you think of it and they believe it feeds another of God's creatures.

From there we went to Mani Bhavan, Gandhi's home and now a museum. It was amazing, and as we moved through reading his works, including a letter to Hitler and President Roosevelt during World War II, and viewing the photos, a sense of serenity passed through all of us. His was such a simple and noble life and so very remarkable. He initiated the spark of independence from British rule.

We then went to Dhobi Ghats, the outdoor laundry. No one does their own laundry in Bombay, but we watched in fascination as men washed and beat the clothes on stone partitions and dried and ironed them. You are sure to have spotlessly clean clothes, but the buttons were to be shattered for sure.

It was time for a bathroom stop and a cool drink away from the hot sun, so we went to the Taj Mahal Hotel, a 5-star establishment. Such opulence in the midst of such poverty is jarring. Wonders, they had western toilets; oh, joy! We rested for about a half hour with Cokes and water—no ice, remember, because it's their own water frozen, not bottled water for ice, and I've had my share of GI problems along the way. We then went to the Colaba Causeway Market, which was great fun, and I was able to do some real bargaining. Our table friends applaud just how far I've come in my bargaining talents. We're getting quite good and got two beautifully carved Indian elephants for the price of one.

After five hours, it was time to go back to the ship. We needed lunch and more water, as it was sweltering and the taxi was small and very cramped. Had a bite to eat and then got ready for Palm Sunday service at 5:00 p.m. After the service, we then had dinner seated with our table friends. To bed early tonight because we get up at 2:00 a.m. tomorrow morning to fly to the Taj Mahal. Can't wait.

Monday, March 17 – The Taj Mahal

We were up at 2:00 a.m. today. Bob called at 2:30 a.m. to make sure we made it. We didn't eat breakfast, as the ship had a goodie bag waiting for us before we boarded our buses to the airport. On dock at the gangway, Bruce, our cruise director and his staff of ten assistants were there to wave us off at 3:30 a.m. in their bathrobes, jammies, curlers, face masks, pillows, and teddy bears. It was a nice gesture and really funny. We learned that this is the first year HAL has provided this one-day, fourteen-hour (more like eighteen-hour) Taj Mahal trip.

We drove through Mumbai in the wee hours of the morning and saw for real just how many people (whole families) sleep on the sidewalks, doorways, beaches, garbage lots, and every possible place for the night. We couldn't believe it. This was in addition to all the animals, dogs, goats, every kind except the sacred cows, which probably had better accommodations than the people. We arrived at the Mumbai airport, went through security (ladies on one side and men on the other), boarded our Jet Airways plane, and settled in for our two-hour flight to Agra in northern India. Mumbai airport was a lovely, large facility. On our flight we were given a beautiful breakfast that we didn't expect but appreciated.

We then landed at Agra's military airport where we were warned repeatedly that we were not to take photos and that HAL and the US government could not help us if we did and got caught. That certainly put the fear of God and the Indian government into us. These people don't mess around and life appears to be cheap, especially in the traffic here. We then boarded buses for about a half-hour drive to the Taj Mahal. Our guide was excellent with a no-nonsense approach and muscled our group ahead of the crowds in all respects.

Now this magnificent Taj Mahal is one of the New Seven Wonders of the World. There is no exclamation that can do it justice. It is the most beautiful and perfect of any structure in history. It is a tomb-crypt of Mumtaz Mahal, the third and most favored wife of Shah Jahan, emperor of Mughal, India, a monument to love and fidelity. It took twenty-two years to build, with twenty thousand laborers and a thousand elephants. This dear woman died giving birth to the Emperor's fourteenth child. Now, if that's favored, forget it; his other two wives were home free, it seems.

Both the emperor and his wife are buried in the crypt in the basement, with fake crypts on the first floor. This is to avoid grave robbers. Everything is absolutely symmetrical, even the trees; but being there defies description. Just as seeing the photograph of a beautiful and perfect woman cannot compare to the experience of seeing her in real life, the Taj Mahal is as magical in person as everyone has said. It is exquisite and as I walked through the arched gateway, I could only gasp at the sight before me. It was breathtaking and a dream come true. This, indeed, was worth the whole world cruise. Sharing this with Bob and Jacquie, who in their generosity made sure we were here, Dick and Jean and Gary and Lona is a memory that will be ours always.

We were able to be at the Taj for an hour and a half, taking pictures from every possible angle, pictures of each other and having our bus group and professional pictures taken with the Taj as a background. Then one last look as we left and headed back through innumerable beggars, hawkers, and animals to our buses. They asked us not to stop but go directly with our guide or we would never get to our buses as a group. As we drove back out of the Taj area with its crush of humanity, we actually saw on the road an Asian elephant, a camel with a load on its back and pulling a cart, donkeys, goats, many dogs who looked better fed than the humans and probably were, water buffalo, and, of course, cows everywhere—sacred as they are in India.

Our guide then took us to a fabulous Indian buffet luncheon at the Sheridan India, another five-star attraction. They go all out to impress us Americans, and they sure do. After lunch we were taken to an extremely interesting shopping area where marble work was done by the same family for generations as far back as when the Taj was built four hundred years ago. This family did the marble and gemstone work on the Taj, and we all sat around the men who were chipping the marble, grinding the gemstones, and adhering them to the indented areas being chipped away. Of course, these fabulous pieces could be purchased. There were tabletops, vases, statues, wall pieces, boxes and containers—everything you could think of made from marble. Also in this shop were embroidered wall hangings, purses, and belts in gold and gemstones on velvet. Magnificent pieces, and with my weakness for purses, I did buy a purse and belt set. Can't wait to wear it on formal night. Outside of this workshop building, workers were in the process of creating the same marble work on the outside of the building, with panels on the sides and over the doorways. It will be spectacular when it is completed.

We then went back to the Sheraton Hotel, our base of operations, to rest and use the best in Agra washrooms that even in a five-star hotel, were not on par with Western facilities at all.

Some of the toilets did not flush properly, and the fixtures were at C status. Amazing where wealth is concentrated. It is opulent, but not always functional in Asian society. We do try not to judge by Western standards. However, sometimes it's impossible.

We left the hotel to go back to Agra's military airport and waited about an hour for our plane to arrive. We got settled and ready for our flight, where we were served another unexpected magnificent meal that was, again, greatly appreciated. By the time we had arrived back in Mumbai and boarded our buses and driven the hour back to the "mother" ship, it was about nine o'clock, and we expected to see many more sleeping people. However, it was an almost carnival atmosphere with all the shops open, people milling about as if it was two in the afternoon. Then we realized: *This is India. They are probably sleeping at two in the afternoon.* No one in their right mind is out in the sun then except mad dogs and Englishmen—and Americans. We arrived at the ship at 10:00 p.m. almost comatose and stumbled to our cabins and bed. The journal had to wait until the next day. It was a day to remember forever.

Tuesday, March 18

Today is a sea day and a rest day. Jack was up and at his class at 9:00 a.m. I slept until 10:00 a.m. Where does he get his energy? He reported that there was a full house today and some new folks. It was a good class, and it's so diverse. After lunch we read and worked on the computer.

Tonight was party night as the ship celebrated St. Patrick's Day a day late because it was a big, big shore day yesterday. Jack and I were invited after dinner to a fun party in the Crow's Nest given by several couples. We met a lovely young lady who is an Indian jewelry designer. She is an American from Miami Beach and also lives outside Bombay. She hires Indian jewelers to make her jewelry and will unveil her collection tomorrow night. She was a delight, and we hope to see her again soon. We enjoyed talking about jewelry, and she knew the marble works and jewelry store in Agra well.

We also met Sheila and Bob Gan and talked about Israel. They go back to Israel every other year. For all Jews it's "next year in Jerusalem." Much has changed since we were there in 1986, and Jack and I really hope to be asked to do the Mediterranean Cruise some year, as it stops in Jerusalem for several days.

We went to the show with an Irish comedian and singer. She and her husband were fun and very talented. It was a good and restful day. It is another sea day tomorrow and then Shalalah, Oman. Looking forward to this, as it has much biblical history.

Wednesday, March 19

Today was a pleasantly warm sea day with calm seas. Jack's class was really well attended with about a hundred people. We are in Holy Week, and people appreciated the opportunity for study and worship because when you are on a ship, it's hard to tell one day from another. Even Sundays are packed with activity. We depend on the days displayed on the carpets in the elevators. Funny, but true.

After class I attended a port lecture on Safaga, Egypt, and Luxor and the Valley of the Kings. Fascinating ancient country and culture. After the port lecture, I attended a lecture by a former diplomat specializing in intercultural and international issues. His topic was the Jewish and Christian influences on Islam, and it helped to know the differences between Sunni and Shiite Islam. It was at the beginning only a geographical difference but then grew to include differences in political views. There is a lot in all three religions that is the same, and there are radical factions in each. Interesting.

After lunch we rested and then got ready for a special dinner at the Pinnacle Grill with Jacque and Bob. HAL gave us a complimentary dinner at this lovely special dining room for four because we had to move from our cabin so that a passenger could be there. It was a sort of thank-you for our trouble. It was appreciated and fun to be with these good friends. Jack and I then went to the show in the Queen's Lounge of the MS *Amsterdam* singers and dancers, and they did a great job. What energy these people have. Tomorrow we dock in Oman, and we have a tour to see many sites. It'll be interesting and another exotic port to explore.

Thursday, March 20

Today at 6:00 a.m. we docked at the port of Salalah, Oman. It's the second largest city in the sultanate of Oman. It is next to Yemen and east of Saudi Arabia. It's the land of the Arabian knights and Sinbad the Sailor in literature. It is basically a desert, and now, during the dry season, it's all sandy and brown with camels everywhere roaming all over the terrain. Supposedly it's the resting place of the biblical Job and also of Nabi Imran, according to legend the father of Mary, mother of Jesus. We saw both tombs. These are probably just legend or a place of remembrance.

We boarded our buses and went first to the impressive Al Hosn Palace, home of the sultan of Oman who overthrew his father in 1970 because the country was in such disruption. It is an absolute monarchy and the people love him. The palace and most of the architecture is so very Arabian looking with beautiful onion domes painted blue and gold. Of the population, 88 percent are Muslim, and the remainder represent many other religions. The people were very friendly and nice, and the nation is one of the US's staunch allies in the world. They have great wealth from oil, but it will last only twenty years unless they find more, and they are trying. The previous commodity of producing wealth is the export of frankincense used in most major religions as incense offering to God or the gods.

Our guide took us to a wonderful souk or marketplace where all the most Arabian looking things were for sale. It was such fun, and even though their currency is about $2.50 to our $1, things were still very inexpensive and beautifully made. After stopping at Mary's father's tomb with bare feet and head scarves needed, we drove out into the hills of Oman. This is pure desert that is extremely hot and dry; boy, did we appreciate an air-conditioned bus. There were interesting little villages in the hills and camels everywhere (one-humped ones). They are branded and belong to people. Many are bred for milk and racing. We have the greatest pictures of them. Saw a flock of about fifty goats being herded by a young boy looking straight out of the first century. Also were many cows and cattle. There is no agriculture because of the dry conditions followed by monsoons, and all their commodities are imported. They are wealthy and putting that wealth into the infrastructure of the country in good roads, public buildings, and utilities for the population. Other areas, as in Dubai farther north, are putting it into opulence so that everyone has magnificent cars but no good roads to drive them on. Gorgeous homes but no sewage systems. Strange what people value.

We went to Job's tomb. Oman is building a tourist industry and wanted to be able to take people to something religious and decided that since other surrounding countries have a Job's tomb, they could too. Of course, everyone claims theirs to be the real one. Another place for bare feet and head scarves, and the tomb attendant didn't feel that I was covered enough so gave me a large green shawl to wrap around me. We then went to the Mughsayl caves and beaches and saw the beautiful coastline of Oman. It was spectacular from above, and the caves were so jutting and unusual in shape. The water was a teal green similar to the Caribbean Sea. Cool and lovely and quite a drive into the hills. At the top our bus began to have gear shift problems, so we had to stop periodically to let them cool. We were very far up and it was quite scary to think our bus was having problems.

Finally we reached the valley and the frankincense trees. We bought a large bag of frankincense and saw that it is a hard amber-like gum resin on the tree that is dried and sold for incense and perfumes. It gives off a sweet perfumed aroma and can even be eaten. However, it's like eating perfume. Yuck! A friend bought some myrrh as well and gave me a jar of it. These two substances were extremely valuable—the same as gold—so it is understandable that these were brought as the most precious gifts possible to the baby Jesus. I'm not sure what substance myrrh is but will do some research on it. At the frankincense trees our bus had problems again and couldn't get up an incline. We all got off the bus, walked the short way to the main road and let the bus get up the hill empty. He made it to all of our applause. We got back on and made it to the ship late for lunch, but happy to have seen such strange, yet beautiful and interesting sites. It was so clean and scrubbed looking and quite a contrast from India.

Had a great dinner sharing with our table friends, only Jacque and Bob didn't make it back in time. Then we went to a show called "Black Tie." They are a very musical family and great entertainers. It was a really good day and such fun.

Hello again, dear ones:

It was a fabulous week with Easter and all the activities involved and especially the Suez Canal and the pyramids. It's hard to believe we have been on board for three months and have only one more month to go. Time is going much too quickly, and we know we may never see some good friends again. We are celebrating every chance we get.

We begin our fourth leg of the journey, and we will have seven ports of call in ten days. It will be exhausting but wonderful. Tomorrow we arrive in Istanbul, Turkey, and all of us are looking so forward to the Grand Bazaar which everyone says is amazing. You can buy anything in the world there. There are many great events coming up that I will love to tell you about throughout the week.

Love to all of you,

Joyce and Jack

JOURNAL # 12

Friday, March 21, 2008 – Good Friday

Busy day today. Jack's class continues to hold at about a hundred persons. He talked about crucifixion, Rome's means of punishment for special criminals who threatened Rome's authority. It was a horror. After class both Jack and I went to the port lecture by Barbara on Alexandria and the Giza pyramids. It'll be wonderful. I then went to a lecture by Dr. Palshikar, an Indian-American who spoke about the caste system in contemporary India. He was excellent and explained how democracy has influenced India in such a way that people wish to be classed in a lower caste for political seats and greater opportunities for education. It is more of an affirmative action turn with the more highly educated and wealthier Brahman caste being unable to have a voice in politics or space in the Indian universities. However, the caste system is alive and well in India as well as in the US. Interesting concepts. We had a lunch date with Jack and Lorraine, a lovely couple in our class. We talked for two hours and really enjoyed our time together.

The afternoon was for working on the computer, and then Jack went to the Good Friday service at 5:00 p.m. There were over 150 attending. A full house. Had dinner and we were all together tonight. We certainly never are bored with our table group, and we have such fun. Came to our cabin after dinner and answered emails and sent out the latest journal installment. Tomorrow is another sea day, and we are looking forward to it.

We turn back our clocks an hour tonight.

Saturday, March 22

Today we are at sea and we have now left the Arabian Sea and sailing in the Red Sea. We've been able to see land today—islands off the coast of Egypt. We have Africa on our port side and Saudi Arabia on our starboard side.

Jack's class was tremendously interesting, and he talked about the progression in the Old Testament of the Jewish concept of life after death. It culminated in the New Testament with Jesus's death and resurrection for Christians as a reality. It was a fascinating study.

It was a quietly restful day with no lectures, so reading in a nice deck chair on a very warm deck was in order for me while Jack worked on his sermons and services for tomorrow. He will have four services beginning at 6:30 a.m. and ending at twelve midnight. It was a good dinner sharing time with our table friends, and then we went to a magic show in the lounge. He was fun to watch and enjoy. We turn our clocks back another hour tonight and get ready for a very busy Easter Day tomorrow.

Sunday, March 23, 2008 – Easter Day

Today it was a thrill to have sunrise services on the top deck in the Red Sea, with Mecca only fifty miles away in Arabia to our right. The top deck was full with hundreds of people, and it was the very first sunrise service I have made in forty-seven years. Sunset is more in tune with my body clock, but this was a never-to-be-repeated experience, and I didn't want to miss it. Father Bill gave the sermon with Jack leading the service since this is really a Protestant tradition. It was a good and memorable experience, and then we just went inside to the Lido and had breakfast with Jacquie and Bob afterward.

At 9:00 a.m. we had the Easter service in the Queen's Lounge with several hundred people attending there as well. Jack's sermon was helpful for understanding the resurrection. We were invited afterwards to a marvelous Easter brunch hosted by Mrs. Wolfe, one of the ladies who threw the Valentine's Day party. The brunch was delicious, and we met a whole new set of people we hadn't before. We sat and enjoyed talking with two Spanish-speaking couples. The two men spoke perfect English, and the one lady could speak a little, but the other lady's husband translated our conversation to and from her. They were delightful people and made me sorry that I'm not bilingual. If I had only some basic Spanish and French, it would be so much easier to get around the world and communicate with others. I realized how important in our global relations languages will be for our grandchildren. After brunch I attended Barbara's port lecture on Istanbul, Turkey. We will be there for two days, and what a treat. That is where our fourth and final leg of our voyage begins. Can't believe we've been on board for three months already.

We rested, and then Jack napped because he has two more services for the crew tonight. We then went to dinner and formal night and the dining room was decorated beautifully with huge paper Easter eggs, balloons, and streamers in Easter colors. Even the Easter bunny joined us. Our menu was much in the traditional line of Easter foods with ham, dyed eggs, and chocolate in many, many forms—yummy. It was all delicious. After dinner, we went to the show to see a very funny comedian, Jason Chase. Mr. Chase had attended the Easter service this morning and introduced himself to us. Several of the officers and crew and entertainers were at the service as well. Jack is now at the crew services and will be back at midnight.

We dock in Safaga, Egypt, at 6:00 a.m. tomorrow. Jack and I plan to just go on shore on our own to explore and enjoy this port of Egypt. It was a wonderful Easter Day, one we will remember always.

Monday, March 24

Today is a beautiful hot, sunny day and we have landed in Safaga. Jack and I decided to stay on board. After breakfast I went to a hair appointment, which was a must. My hair grows so quickly in hot weather. We then attempted to catch the shuttle into town from the dock into the Holiday Inn Hotel and shops nearby, just to say we were on Egyptian soil. When we went through customs, there was no shuttle. They had sent only one, and there would have been an hour's wait for it to return. Out on deck we could see a small town, with beautiful roads and highways, but no cars on them. Only a few trucks and buses. Strange to be sure. We then went in to lunch and decided to stay put and rest after a very busy Easter Day of services, parties, and dinners. We needed to just sit in deck chairs and vegetate.

Today was also a marathon Run for the Cure, and the First Officer of Culinary, Bert, ran twenty-six miles in the hot Egyptian desert sun to raise funds for the Komen Foundation. I understood he raised over $5,000 toward our goal of $50,000 for this Golden Anniversary Voyage. I received word this week that my Aunt Gloria, my dad's sister-in-law, died last week, and we were able to give a donation to cancer research in her memory. As we were so far from home, it helped to remember her in this way. We were glad we were on deck to be able to cheer for Bert as he came onto the Safaga dock. It was such fun with all the pink balloons, pink lemonade served, our captain greeting him, and the MS *Amsterdam* band playing upon his last stretch toward the ship. He had a great welcome celebration.

After dinner we saw the wonderful movie *August Rush*. It was a happily-ever-after story and a real feel-good movie. We set sail at midnight tonight after all the passengers who toured Luxor, Valley of the Kings, have returned back on ship, and we will head toward the mouth of the Suez Canal. It'll be so exciting to have sailed both the Panama Canal and Suez Canal on the same grand voyage. Next year the World Cruise won't be going by way of the canals again so we were really lucky to be on ship this year. It was a good, restful day, and we took lots of pictures from the deck. Another sea day tomorrow.

Tuesday, March 25

Today was a beautiful summer's day—warm and breezy, with calm seas. It was a busy morning with Jack's class. Not as many people today, as many of our group went to Luxor and the Valley of the Kings yesterday and didn't get back until midnight. Can't blame them for sleeping in. They had a wonderful time. Jack spoke about the Sadducees' concept of no life after death and the Pharisees' concept of life after death and their questioning Jesus about it.

After class, I went to the port lecture on Sochi, Russia. I'm glad we signed up for a tour in Sochi as we would not be able to get off the ship otherwise. People would have had to get a Russian visa before leaving the US to be able to go on shore on their own. Only four persons on board have the proper visa and can do so, and it is a very complicated and expensive process. We, however, will be able to go ashore with a tour group.

I then went to a lecture by Dr. Palshikar explaining some of the more popular deities in Hinduism. Very fascinating; I was surprised to learn that Hindus believe in one God but in many forms. Therefore, they have thousands of god forms to whom they personally pray, and having idols is not prohibited for them.

They even worship Mary, the mother of Jesus. They're not at all picky about whom they worship, but they universally know they are basically worshiping one God in whatever form they choose. Amazing!

Had lunch and then took the opportunity to press our clothes. I'm going to feel like tossing my whole travel wardrobe when I get home, as I'm getting quite sick of them all. Picking up a new top here and there does help.

Had dinner and learned about Jean, Dick, Bob, and Jacquie's tour to the Valley of the Kings. Hope we have another chance to come to Egypt again to do this particular tour. It sounded terrific. We'll see the oldest pyramids at Giza on Thursday. Went to the "Black Tie" show tonight, and what a talented family. It was so enjoyable.

Beginning at 6:30 a.m. tomorrow we will sail through the Suez Canal for twelve hours, with Barbara giving commentary. Right now we are anchored in the Gulf of Suez and will be in the first convoy to start through tomorrow. Cruise ships have priority to go through, except for military, and it costs a ship $200,000. *Wow!* But what a thrill to be doing this.

Wednesday, March 26

Today at 6:30 a.m. we began with the first convey through the Suez. It was a real celebration on deck, with special rolls and coffee served before breakfast. The apricot cheese rolls were delicious. We travel between the Eastern Desert on our left and the Sinai Peninsula on our right. Egypt owns this canal, and it is a very, very strategic military stronghold. We couldn't believe the numbers of armed troops protecting this complete stretch. We entered at the Gulf of Suez and ended at Port Said. It was all pure desert with no locks, as the elevation is the same on each end. It was to take up to twelve hours, but we got through in eight and a half. There were some oases and cities along the way, but basically the countryside is wasteland.

We have now been through both major canals in the world. The Panama is in the jungle and the Suez in the desert. How exactly opposite they are, and both are such landmarks. One fun fact I learned is that Verdi wrote the opera *Aida* to commemorate the opening of the Suez. However, the opera was completed two years later. Now I know why there is a caravan of elephants in the opera.

We entered the Mediterranean at about 4:30 p.m. and are now on our way to Alexandria. We are expected to dock tomorrow at 4:30 a.m., and our tour to the Giza Necropolis leaves at 5:45 a.m. We, therefore, came right back to our cabin after dinner and prepared for tomorrow's big day. It will be an exciting day, and we'll be up at 3:00 a.m. tomorrow. We can sleep the next day. What a joy to see the pyramids, but the greater joy is that we are so fortunate to be there.

Thursday, March 27

We are in Alexandria, Egypt. This great city was conquered by Alexander the Great in 332 BC. Most of the ancient city is either covered over with more modern buildings on top or else underwater. We boarded our buses at 5:30 a.m. to begin our journey through Alexandria City into Cairo and Giza Necropolis (City of the Dead); of the seven ancient wonders of the world, Giza is the only one remaining.

We passed the site of the lighthouse on the island of Pharos in the Alexandria harbor. It was also one of the seven ancient wonders but is now a fort. The lighthouse was destroyed in an earthquake in the first century and then completely razed shortly after by another. We also passed the famous library, now a beautiful modern structure designed by a Norwegian architect.

The first library, a great ancient university and medical school, was tragically burned. Our guide told us that although they know of the treasures underwater at the harbor, they are unable at this time to bring them up because they have been in salt water so long that the chemical reaction with the earth's atmosphere causes great and rapid deterioration. They are attempting to develop a huge glass tube under the harbor so that people will be able to walk underwater to see the treasurers. I hope I see that day.

We rode for three hours to Cairo and the pyramids past lush farmlands irrigated by water from the Nile River. There were lots of donkeys and carts working the beautiful fields. The vegetation is only along the snakelike Nile; the rest of the land mass is desert only. Lots and lots of desert. Cairo is a large Egyptian city with modern architecture and not particularly pretty but very square with some lovely arches and domes on public buildings, hotels, and resort complexes. Egypt is a fairly wealthy nation, with some oil resources. There was a large population of Jewish and Greek people prior to the wars with Israel. There were once ten thousand Jewish people but now less than five hundred. Cairo, with a population of twenty-seven million people, is a very crowded, noisy, but clean city. There are many monuments in public squares. The Nile runs through it and is very beautiful and serene looking, with lush trees and gardens along the way.

Our first stop was the Egyptian Museum of Antiquities and exhibits all the treasures of King Tutankhamen (Tut). He was a boy king at nine years old and died of gangrene at the age of twenty. As he was getting out of his chariot, he broke his knee, and the infection was never discovered until it was too late. He died a horrible death and was in a coma for nine months. Amazing what they can tell from a mummy. I was surprised to learn that his tomb was in Luxor, the Valley of the Kings, and not Giza near Cairo where his treasure is displayed. It was one of the only tombs that had the treasure intact and not molested by grave robbers.

Our guide was phenomenal and was an Egyptologist who

really knew her subject well. Her enthusiasm was contagious and made our tour spectacular. She guided us through the museum telling us exactly how a corpse was mummified as we leaned casually against a huge stone table for preparing mummies in the center of the exhibition. The highlight was the solid gold funerary mask of King Tut, the most precious of the treasures, capping the display in a special room through which we moved shoulder to shoulder in mass. This was incredible to see, and only here did we see the magnitude of it all.

After a very short hour and a half there, we boarded our buses to do a little shopping in Giza in a magnificent souk. Jack and I wandered off, not interested in any more jewelry, gold, or brasses and found a wonderful little art gallery with paintings on papyrus. We found a beautiful "Tree of Life" painting for our bedroom that will be perfect with our oriental carpet. Also from one of the hawkers we got a good history book of Egypt cheaper than in the store or museum. Surprisingly, the hawkers don't intimidate us anymore, and we sometimes enjoy the banter and fun of haggling.

We were taken to another gorgeous five-star hotel, the Mena House Oberoi, once a palace, in Giza for a delicious buffet of all native Egyptian foods. Finally, after waiting for so long, we were taken to the great Giza pyramids. We could get glimpses of them as we traveled into Giza. Can't hide a humungous pyramid. But our bus went right up to the base of the largest one. I was spellbound by its size and grandeur. Not only did we take loads of pictures of the pyramids, but we also took pictures of each other with Jacquie, Bob, Gary, and Lona with us. There were hawkers, bazaars at the base, and camel drivers wanting you to ride and/or take pictures (for a price, of course). Who would imagine we would have so much fun in a graveyard, and our weather was perfect—sunny, seventy-five or eighty degrees, with a slight breeze. It was actually pleasant to be outside in the blazing sun.

We went to the great Sphinx, which was huge and really impressive. It was at the temple of funeral preparation for burial.

These were the oldest pyramids, 5,000 years old. Our guide also told us that recent excavations have discovered the City of the Workers. Those who built the pyramids were not slaves at all, but very well paid artesans who worked on royal tombs. They found information on what they were paid and shift schedules for the workers. We have many misconceptions of the ancients, it seems.

We then boarded our buses reluctantly for our long three-hour trip back to the mother ship and home. We arrived back fourteen hours from when we left but light years smarter and more informed about Egypt, the pyramids, and the delightful, friendly people we met along the way—especially our wonderful guide, Dina. She was the very best we have had yet.

We ate a quick dinner at the Lido. The dining room stayed open for dinner so that our group could eat a regular dinner upon our return. Then to bed, exhausted but happy. Tomorrow is a sea day and hopefully rest.

Hi, everyone!

Another amazing week with such marvelous ports. Carme, our terrific entertainer this week, did sing that great song that Louis Armstrong sang, "It's a Wonderful World." It is, dear ones, it is, and I thank God for my time in history right now to see just how wonderful it truly is.

All of you please have a blessed week.

Love,

Joyce and Jack

JOURNAL # 13

Friday, March 28

It is a good, restful sea day today. We're in the Mediterranean Sea along the coast of Turkey, and tomorrow we dock in Istanbul on the Black Sea. It's getting colder, and all our officers are wearing their sharp-looking navy wool uniforms instead of their summer whites we've seen the whole cruise. After the 80s and 90s in Africa and Asia, it's now in the low 50s, so the sweaters and jackets come out again.

I slept until 10:00 a.m., and it felt good. I seem to have caught up from Cairo's adventures. Jack had worship this morning because Sunday we will be touring in Istanbul, with a huge reception in the evening in the Istanbul cisterns with HAL's CEO and his wife and entourage. I cannot imagine having a gala party in a "cistern," but we shall find out. All the guests plus we who are staff are being bused there for the event. Then the CEO and entourage will be on board with us for several days until we get to Sochi, Russia. There will be thirty to forty buses available to do the transferring to the cisterns.

I attended the port lecture on Sevastopol, Ukraine, this afternoon and then worked on the computer until time to dress for dinner. Tonight the theme was "Aladdin - Istanbul night." Some of the outfits people wore were beautiful Egyptian formal wear. Many, both men and women got lovely clothes at the bazaars yesterday while in Egypt—the men in flowing robes and headdresses and the ladies in scarves with gold coins and dangling headpieces. Even some belly dancers with a bit too much "belly." It was fun and the pictures will be great to see.

After dinner we went to the MS *Amsterdam* singers and dancers' show called "Songs of the South." They are very talented young folks. Then to bed for tomorrow, as we dock in Istanbul at about 11:00 a.m. We have an afternoon tour and the Grand Bazaar. Can't wait to see what this adventure will be in such an exotic port of call.

Saturday, March 29

We are in Istanbul, and is it ever wonderful. We sailed into the harbor at 10:30 a.m., and what a photo op that was with all of the magnificent mosques' domes and minarets on the skyline. It wasn't bright sunny weather but partially sunny, yet still enough for good photos. It was cold today and quite windy on the waterfront. We had a leisurely breakfast, picked up lira currency and our passports from the front office, and prepared to go on our tour at 1:00 p.m. after lunch.

We went ashore and boarded our buses for a tour of the Old City History and Grand Bazaar. Our guide, Omar, was a young Turkish gentleman who spoke perfect English. He was very knowledgeable and funny, a pure delight. Our first stop was the Grand Bazaar of Istanbul. That is a total experience. There were 4,400 stores in a covered area of more than sixty streets. All beautifully kept, clean and tidy—no litter anywhere—and even Western toilets. The shopkeepers were friendly, encouraging but not overbearing, and Jack and I had a delightful hour and a half shopping, looking, and talking with the people and shopkeepers. We have never seen anything quite like this. We hated to leave; it was such fun, and we were very credible in our bargaining.

The Turkish tiles are lovely and the cashmere scarves elegant—soft, with beautiful colors and designs. Jack even got the evil eye necklace as a fun thing for our table friends. We have become quite adept at graciously refusing carpet sellers. They are everywhere and very persuasive and charming. Our friend Lona even had two proposals of marriage in the bargaining process. Gary, her husband, is beginning to take this seriously and may up the ante on her value somewhat. How boring it will be to just shop at regular mall prices at home. Shopping in the East is an art form.

We reluctantly boarded our buses and went to the area of the gorgeous Blue Mosque and Hagia Sofia. For 1,000 years it was a Christian church, then for five hundred years an Islamic mosque; now it is a lovely museum. We also viewed the Turkish public baths. The architecture is all one would expect in Turkey, especially the exciting, exotic international city of Istanbul, where you see the onion domes, minarets and hear the call to prayer over the city five times a day. The city is 99 percent Muslim but very westernized in dress, mostly Sunni and very progressive. We saw very few in native dress, unlike India, Oman, and Egypt. We did see, however, many Muslim women in burkas. This is a black or brown covering from head to toe, but no veils just some scarves. We did not go into these historic sights because it was just a highlights tour. Tomorrow we will go with friends on a private tour and get into all these fabulous places and take more inside pictures. At this point we have several thousand pictures. Thank God for digital, and we picked up another, better camera in Hong Kong.

Our guide then took us back to our bus where we went for a complete windshield tour of the old city. The ancient walls of the city are still intact. There's some destruction from earthquakes, but a lot still stands, with wonderful arches and gates into the old city. The lower parts of the walls are from the first century and the upper parts slightly later, about the fifth century. They are amazing. The gardens were beautiful, with tulips, the symbol of the Ottoman Empire, and pansies in every possible piece of earth throughout the city. Next to the ancient walls people have planted huge vegetable gardens, and some set up little stands to sell their fresh produce. The tulip really came from Istanbul and was then taken to Holland. It is a Turkish flower first. Istanbul is a huge city of seventeen million people with a wonderful blend of the old and new. It is the only city in the world on two continents, Europe and Asia, with the Bosporus waterway separating it. We remained on the European side where all the historic sites and the Grand Bazaar and exotic Spice Market are located. Tomorrow we will explore even more.

We came back to the ship about 4:30 p.m. and had dinner. All of our table friends were there except Bob and Jacquie. Tomorrow is Sunday, but because of all the events going on, church was held yesterday morning instead. There is a very special event occurring because this is the Golden Anniversary of HAL's World Voyages, and the CEO will be entertaining us along with the US ambassador to Turkey, Mr. Ross Wilson. It will be a grand affair, and we look forward to it. We set our clocks one hour forward tonight so we lose an hour's sleep. It will be a stellar day tomorrow in Istanbul. We love it here.

Sunday, March 30

Our second day in Istanbul, and what a wonderful day it has been. We met our friends at 9:00 a.m. for our private tour. Our guide, Yaman, was a very well-educated and informed young man who was an English major in college but has been a licensed tour guide for eighteen years. He told us much more than we learned yesterday.

We began our tour at the Hippodrome where the chariot races used to be held in the Byzantine era. There in the oval center, was a Roman obelisk and one also that was from Egypt with carvings all over it. We entered the Museum of Turkish and Islamic Arts, which has the most extensive collection of Turkish rugs in the world. We learned the difference between Kilim weaving, which has a very smooth finish with no knots, and a knotted handmade rug, which is tufted and quite plush in texture. The colors all from natural dyes were still brilliant and beautifully blended. Many were mosque rugs that were huge and intricately made.

Our next stop was the Sultan Ahmed Mosque or we know it as the Blue Mosque. This was built a mere four hundred years ago in 1603, and they consider it modern. We removed our shoes and covered our heads (ladies) and entered into the most magnificent display of tiles imaginable. It is called Blue Mosque because as you enter, the sun coming through the blue stained glass windows and reflecting on the predominately blue tiles creates a bluish haze inside the worship area. It is a lovely and worshipful sight. There was a very striking gold tower with many step up to it where the Qu`ran is read and preached.

We then went to the Topkapi Palace. An amazing structure, a city unto itself really, built by the Sultan Mehmet II in 1453 after he sacked Constantinople. Islam has reigned from that time on. Many Sultans after him enlarged and embellished this gorgeous area. The opulence of the jewels, tiles, and artworks was astounding. In the treasury we saw the jewels, including the Spoonmaker's Diamond, which weighs 86 carats. It was told that an old pauper found this diamond in a trash heap and sold it to a dealer for three wooden spoons. It has since been called the Spoonmaker's Diamond. On several thrones we saw emeralds the size of baseballs. This would put the Royal English Crown Jewels to shame.

But what was most fun was the harem. The word *harem* in Islam derives from a word (*haram*) meaning "forbidden." So for Muslims, alcohol would be haram. The first harem in this palace was built for 114 women—four official wives (only four allowed), along with several "favorites" and many concubines. Concubines were beautiful slave girls with the heady ambition to become a favorite and then possibly a wife. The harem in later times housed over four hundred women but not all for the sultan's pleasure. They were daughters, sisters, and all female relatives. The sultan's mother was the queen bee of it all. The women's quarters had eunuchs as overseers. They were usually black Africans because, grossly enough, they seemed to be the ones strong enough to survive the grisly castration process. The rooms were of course amazing, with the characteristic tiles, domes, couches and other furniture, and artwork. The Turkish government is in the process of restoring much of the harem, and not all of the rooms were open.

By this time, our group was dying of hunger, and our guide relented and allowed us back to our van for lunch. We scarfed down the peanut butter and jelly sandwiches we'd quickly made at breakfast and in ten minutes we were ready to go again. We then went to the Hagia Sofia, now a gorgeous museum. This was a basilica first built in AD 360 and burned and rebuilt in AD 404; then it burned again and was rebuilt in AD 532. It was full of the most mind-boggling mosaics, friezes, tiles, and frescos. All of this had been plastered over when it became a mosque after a thousand years as a Christian church. Muslims did this because in their religion, they cannot depict any living form. Much of the white plaster has been removed, but some can't be removed without damage to the tiles beneath it. It is now a museum of great pride for Turkey and Istanbul. It was the largest church in the world until St. Peter's in Rome was built. Our last stop was to the Basilica Cistern built in AD 532 to provide a water supply for the palace. We entered and went down many steps to an underground arched colonnade that could match any European cathedral. This was spectacular and had over three hundred columns and arches with exotic lighting and Turkish music playing. The water below our walkways were filled with the most interesting fish to eat the algae to keep it clean, and it really was very clean.

After leaving the cisterns, we boarded our lovely van and headed back to the ship. We arrived at 4:00 p.m. and got ready for our early 4:30 p.m. dinner and then preparations to board our buses to the Binbirdirek Cistern for our gala affair with the CEO of Holland America Lines and his wife. This cistern was built in AD 330, even earlier than the Basilica cistern. It is hard for me to conceive something so old. This is before the Roman Empire fell, and the engineering is incredible. I realize just how very new our country and the American civilization really is.

We arrived at the cistern with red, blue and white draperies flowing everywhere with "Welcome Holland America Golden Grand Voyage" banners at the entrance looking like a sultan's tent. As we each walked through the hall to be presented to the president of HAL, a Turkish band was playing beautiful, swaying rhythms. The photographers were taking pictures of us, and all the ship's officers were standing in attendance. It was the most beautiful and elegant experience we've ever had. We crowded into a huge stone arched and columned area draped with colored fabrics on the walls, and all the tables, chairs, benches, couches, and stools were covered in pristine white fabric with purple and white flowers and candles everywhere. It felt as if we were entering a magnificent Arabian Nights cave. The floor was many platforms constructed over the water deep below.

Immediately, waiters presented us with food and drink. Shortly after we arrived, the entertainment began with three stages positioned throughout the huge room including closed circuit TVs around the walls as well. The first were dancers presenting a native spondaic in colorful costumes of ancient dress and after that more food was served with beverages flowing freely. We then were treated to a fire breather (or fire eater). They used torches of fire to put into their mouths and then after putting lighter fluid in their mouths breathed out great volumes of fire that sent flames and sparks and heat out many, many feet into the audience. It was both exciting and chilling to watch them perform. There were then other novelty dancers with faces painted on their torsos and then came the highlight of the evening: the belly dancers. *Wow!*

What beautifully endowed ladies they were. If anything would get a royal sultan's blood raging, these ladies sure would, and were they ever flexible and smooth in their movements. Fascinating! Then came the short speeches of our CEO, Ambassador Wilson, the Turkish ambassador, and the Dutch ambassador. I must remember that HAL is a Dutch concern.

We were definitely ready to board our buses, stuffed with delicious food and drink, great music, and marvelous and exciting entertainment—and had good friends to share it. When the MS *Amsterdam* sailed out of Istanbul's harbor that night, a magnificent fireworks display was given in our honor. After touring all day and partying into the night, Jack and I crawled to our cabin, more than ready to hit our pillows in blissful sleep. We didn't make it; on the Lido deck was a dessert extravaganza. Friends told us there was a chocolate fountain, chocolate sculptures, and every sweet treat imaginable. We had no room left for anything more and could hardly pick up a camera to take another picture.

It was a fairy tale day. Two days really, because Istanbul is a fairy tale and magical city. One we pray to see again someday.

Monday, March 31

We were awake at 7:00 a.m. and couldn't believe we were able to walk after yesterday. After a hot breakfast, as the dining room was cold enough to freeze water, I went to Jack's class. Surprisingly, there were about eighty people present. At breakfast, we joked that we would be the only two there. Some of our class members did leave us in Istanbul, as it ended this leg of their journey, and about fifty more passengers arrived on board. There were about six new members in the class today. Jack talked about the meaning of the twenty-third Psalm and the passage, "You prepare a table before me in the presence of my enemies" (verse 5, NRSV), in relation to the meaning of Mideastern hospitality and commitment to guests and their safety in their home. So interesting, and a concept quite foreign to us Westerners.

After lunch I attended Barbara's port lecture on Venice, Italy, a port of call in our near future. Came back to our cabin for a rest, and then dressed in formal wear for a cocktail party with the CEO and his wife in the Queen's Lounge. Jack had a good opportunity to thank the CEO for HAL's continuing to provide chaplains on all cruises while other cruise lines are no longer doing so. He replied by stating that HAL will continue to do so in the future. We sure hope so. We then had dinner with our table friends and shared our two days' experiences in Istanbul. After dinner we then went to the show, tonight called Opera Interludes. It was the best opera we have heard in many years. Such great talent, and the artists received many ovations. That is a rare occurrence here as we receive many excellent performers.

Back to our cabin so Jack could rest before going to his 11:00 p.m. service for the crew. Since they all had to work so much later into the night, yesterday's service was changed to tonight instead. Our crew work very hard for us, and appreciate it a great deal. Actually, we want to take them all home with us, since we have forgotten how to cook, clean, do laundry or make a bed. *Ah!*

Tomorrow we dock in Sochi, Russia. We arrive at 8:00 a.m., and we have a great tour planned to a Russian tea plantation and tea house. This is another UNESCO World Heritage Site and is a vacation resort area for Russia's elite. President Bush and Mr. Putin are meeting there on April 5 and 6. Interesting what may be waiting for us as well.

Tuesday, April 1 – April Fool's Day

And we are in Sochi, Russia. We docked at 8:00 a.m. offshore, and it was a port where we were tendered in. Our tour was to begin when tendered but we heard that the immigration officials gave the ship officials a real headache. They were tendered out to our ship and took forever setting up their computers to enter data by hand. Then they wanted snacks delivered to them, after which they asked for more snacks. Then they wouldn't allow anyone to come down the stairs to the gangway but only on the elevators. That took four times as long for everyone to get through immigration procedures. So therefore, our tours were cut by one or two hours. Actually it was hilarious to watch. They had to be doing this "just because."

Sochi is a lovely summer resort area. However, today the temperature was 48 degrees F and so foggy and rainy we could barely see anything outside the bus windows. We had a very nice lady as our guide who knew a great deal about this area and the 2014 Winter Olympics being held at this site. Our tour was the Sochi Sights and Dagomys Tea Tasting. Dagomys was a farming area about an hour's drive from the port, and it is springtime here. Amazingly, it is a subtropical climate. Except for today, of course. There were palm trees and many other trees and flowers in full bloom. It looks like a set from Dr. Zhivago, as it has that perfectly Russian look. We arrived at the tea plantation and were ushered into a tea house, a wooden structure with tables, benches, music, and ladies greeting us in beautiful native costume. We were served the most delicious Russian black tea from huge samovars and very large teapots—along with superb freshly baked sweet yeast breads swirled with poppy seed and some with jam that was heavenly. On the tables were bowls of apples and filbert nuts with nutcrackers. It was such a treat. We then were entertained by several ladies and gentlemen who played Russian instruments and sang folk songs and danced. It was very nice and we stayed about 45 minutes; all made bathroom stops, and then headed back to our buses for the hour's drive back to our ship tenders.

We stopped briefly at the tea fields for pictures. It was especially interesting to see the tea bushes that are about knee high for easy plucking (not picking) of the topmost leaves for harvesting. Russian tea is dried in special stoves giving it a rather strong, smoky flavor and dark color. In other countries teas are air dried. I had attended the lectures on board about the history of tea and its growing and preparation, so this was a good final step in the learning process. We arrived back at our ship to go through customs and immigration again; our poor passports are getting stamped to death, which is a sign of good travels. We had lunch and rested for the remaining afternoon.

After dinner we went to the show of Carme. He is a comedian and singer from Las Vegas and was extremely funny and very good. Back to our cabins to prepare for tomorrow, and we'll dock or actually drop anchor for another tender to Sevastopol, Ukraine. This will be fun, and we'll see the summer palace of Nicholas II and his family. It was a good day, interesting and we can say we've now been on Russian soil.

The entertainer tonight also impersonated Louis Armstrong and sang "It's a Wonderful World," as Satchmo would so beautifully sing. We are all seeing firsthand just what a wonderful world it really is, and we were all deeply touched because we can also see how fragile it is as well.

Wednesday, April 2

We have anchored at the port site of Sevastopol, Ukraine. After breakfast we went through a very brief immigration process. Thank heavens, and boarded our tenders for a half-hour sail into the port. It was a foggy, rainy morning again in the Black Sea giving the impression of this lovely country as rather dark, mystical, misty, and ethereal. We boarded our buses on shore preparing for our two-hour drive to the Crimean Peninsula through the soaring Krymsky Mountains with their jagged peaks and coastline. Our guide, Natasha, spoke great English and was a wealth of information. We drove through huge vineyards where Crimean champagne and sweet dessert wines are produced. Lush farmland and rocky areas. We drove by the battlefields of the Crimean War in Balaclava, home of the "Charge of the Light Brigade," by Alfred Lord Tennyson. There were many new churches being built and much renovation being done on all Christian churches and cathedrals. The blue and gold onion domes and crosses were beautiful even in the foggy mist, which added somewhat to the ambience.

We arrived outside the city of Yalta at a beautiful fairy tale castle perched on a huge rock jutting out of the Black Sea. This was called the Swallow's Nest, a summer dacha for a wealthy government official. It was lovely, and we were taken to lunch at a pretty little restaurant across from the Swallow's Nest. There, we were served a fabulous lunch of the native foods, and at each place was a glass of vodka, table wine, and mineral water. If we were to drink all that, who would care what we ate—or when, for that matter—but it is standard for good restaurants to serve in the Ukraine. Lunch was delicious with lots of it, and we were entertained with music and by dancers in folk dress. Absolutely beautiful costumes. After lunch and shopping we drove into Yalta and Czar Nicholas II's summer palace, Livadia, built in 1911 in the classic style of local white limestone. It was gorgeous, as Russian opulence can be.

We had somehow not made the connection that the 1945 Yalta Conference was held at Livadia Palace; we were thrilled to learn it. Here, Churchill, Roosevelt, and Stalin met to sign the Yalta Agreement at the conclusion of WWII, dividing the spoils, so to speak. The pictures on the walls, the table and chairs where they sat, and the intact room were all there, and I could think how much our son-in-law, John, would have loved to be here with his knowledge and appreciation of WWII history.

The second floor was devoted to the Czar's ill-fated family with family pictures of everyone on the walls. Our guide pointed out that no picture of Rasputin was ever displayed in the castle because even though Czarina Alexandra admired him, the Czar did not and was suspicious of him. However, because he loved and respected Alexandra, he allowed Rasputin to visit the palace. The furnishings and decorations were beautiful and made for a magnificent summer home. The family had only been there four times before their deaths; so sad. DNA studies have verified that all in the family were executed and no one survived, as it was once believed Anastasia had. There have been several pretenders in history, but it was false.

We bought a wonderful original watercolor of the Swallow's Nest castle to take home. We still have no idea how we are going to get all our "stuff" home, but we will, I'm sure. We boarded our buses back to the port to be tendered back to our ship and got there just as the crew was weighing anchor. *Whew!* We then had to wait for other tenders not back yet from Yalta. That evening we had dinner with our table friends. After dinner we went directly to our cabins and bed. Very tired but happy with our wonderfully exciting and unexpected adventures. Tomorrow is a sea day, and we travel through the Dardanelles, the Sea of Marmara, and the Bosporus on our way to Santorini, Greece. We're looking forward to seeing it on Friday.

Thursday, April 3

We are now in the Aegean Sea. Today, a sea day, was one of commentary from our port lecturer as we traveled through the Bosporus, the Sea of Marmara, and the Dardanelles out to the Aegean Sea. We are now heading up the coast of Greece with the city of Troy on our left. Troy is not a mythical city, but for real. It is now called Illium in Turkey. We are heading to the southernmost island of Greece called Santorini.

Jack's class was very interesting, and then we had lunch with friends who are travel agents with Vantage. We discovered they are dear friends of another friend in our summer community, Bay View. It is a very small world indeed. We all made it to dinner tonight and had a great time sharing our Russian and Ukrainian days' adventures.

We then went to the movie, *The Ultimate Gift*, featuring James Garner, who is one of my favorite actors. It's a three-hanky movie and terrific. We changed our currency to euros for our time in Europe, picked up photocopies of our passports, and then were off to bed to be ready for an early tour tomorrow. It's still a thrill to step on foreign soil each time and know that something new is in store for us. It is another new day of adventures tomorrow.

Hi again, everyone:

What a week we have had. Hope you all enjoy this week's installment, and it pains us that there are only two more weeks to go. When we boarded this magnificent ship in January, April seemed very far away, and we wondered if we would be able to stand the long journey. Well, as you can see, we could not only stand it just fine but revel in its glory. We miss our dear family and friends. But we'll be home on the 27th and catch up with everything and everyone really soon. Meanwhile, we tour on and enjoy the four ports we have left.

Have a beautiful week, and we miss you all.

Love to all,

Joyce and Jack

JOURNAL # 14

Friday, April 4

Today at 8:00 a.m. we anchored outside the port of Santorini, Greece, and what a gorgeous skyline. We came into port by Santorini's tenders, as they have a very strong boatman's union and wouldn't allow the MS *Amsterdam* to use our tenders. The Aegean Sea was very rough and choppy, and going ashore was a rather exciting experience itself. There was only a small sea level port area and then sheer rock going 1,800 feet up.

Our buses were waiting for us, and we all knew we were going straight up. We did so in a series of terrifying hairpin curves, with no guardrails and very narrow roads. It was just better to look out at the beautiful blue sea, cliffs, and lovely whitewashed buildings and houses and not what our driver was doing. However, it wasn't as hairy as Manila. We drove past many beautiful and very unusual vineyards. Because of such constant high winds, they are not able to cultivate the vines along arbors but they trained the vines into circles and each grape vine was like a large basket about a foot high and the grapes grew inside the baskets protected from the high winds. Ingenious!

Our first stop after taking scores of picture from this precipice, was a monastery called The Prophet Elias Monastery. The legend was that Elias was a seaman and traveled to Santorini, Greece. Our guide said it's a legend, and this is where we remember him.

Santorini is a volcanic island and one of several surrounding the central volcano out in the Aegean Sea. It is believed by some scientists that this is the lost city of Atlantis. Many, many centuries ago it was one large island, and then the greatest volcanic eruption in the world occurred, with the island exploding and leaving many smaller islands, destroying the civilization that was there. The volcano is currently dormant but potentially active. Scary!

We visited a winery, as there are a thousand grape growers on the island, and the winery was a cooperative. We then drove through the largest town, called Fira Town. People were parked in the middle of the very narrow streets. A car was parked there when our bus was coming through. Our driver laid on his horn until a man came out of a nearby shop and screamed what sounded like dire profanities in Greek to our driver. Of course, our driver returned the compliment, but the car owner went back into the shop. Our driver again leaned on his horn and we waited for the man to finish his business and then calmly drive his car away. It was fun to watch all this erupted drama.

We then went to the beautiful town of Oia and had to walk a long way up a very steep incline which was difficult for some of our elderly passengers. However, it was a perfect view. In the mountains were houses built into the caves. The Greek architecture was lovely and so very simple, clean lines, yet was elegant with rounded roofs and arches. The churches were all white with blue domes, to symbolize heaven, with gold crosses on top. The houses and building are all whitewashed every year by decree of city ordinance. They were busily preparing for the Greek Easter coming later in April. The sun just shone on these sparkling buildings, and they were dazzling. It was picture-postcard beautiful. We took many pictures and of course browsed the lovely shops. Jack bought a wonderful clay bird, beautifully hand molded, and I bought an exquisite scarf for evening wear. The handwork was lovely.

We again boarded our buses for the descent down the mountain. Our driver was cautious and reached the bottom safely. We hated to leave this paradise but reached the tenders and our ship in time for lunch. Rested this afternoon and then had dinner and a show after. A flautist performed, and she was wonderfully talented. Tomorrow is a sea day as we sail our way toward Venice, Italy—a country and city I've longed to visit. We set our clocks back another hour tonight and look forward to a good day tomorrow.

Saturday, April 5

It is a lovely sea day. Jack's class was great. He talked about the twelve apostles of Jesus—who they were, where they came from, and the meaning of their names. It was an extremely interesting revelation.

I attended the port lecture on Split, Croatia, which promises to be a beautiful and interesting port and tour. Jack then joined me for the lecture by Dr. Phillip Harding on "Diocletian the Dalmatian, the Roman Empire in Transition." It was very interesting and informative, especially since we dock in Venice tomorrow. After lunch I exercised and then rested and read until dinner. It was formal night, and everyone looked lovely, even the guys. We then went to the show, and Opera Interludes again performed. They are excellent and their selections were terrific. We hate to see them leave us in Venice. Some of our class members will leave us then as well, and some others will join us. With people coming and going at each leg of the journey, we feel so privileged to have been on for the whole voyage. We have learned so much not only about each wonderful port but living on board a luxury cruise liner. One biggie we have learned is if you eat all that is offered to you, you will be as big as a cruise ship. It's "no desserts" from here on out for both of us.

Tomorrow will be exciting, and we will spend two days in Venice. What a thrill!

Sunday, April 6

We are in beautiful, ancient Venice. Our sail-in was spectacular. The sun was shining on the church domes, spires, and towers of the city, and it was Sunday. As we entered Venice harbor, the bells began to ring the call for church services. It felt as though Venice was greeting us like old friends. Barbara gave us running commentary as we made our way into the city and our berth for docking.

We had our church service today, but it was only twenty minutes long because everyone wanted to be on deck for this glorious sail-in. Jack knew that because we would be here for two days, people would not be coming back to the ship in time for 5:00 p.m. service, so he decided a short morning service would be best. It was appreciated by all.

We had our lunch and then boarded our "boat buses" to take us to the Palazzo Ducale, the doge's (president's) palace. This is now a museum of pink and white mosaic exterior and fabulous Tintoretto and Veronese murals decorating the walls, ceilings, and every possible corner and crevice. It was the center of government for the republic and was built in the ninth century. It is connected by the "bridge of sighs" over a canal to the prison. This was the first prison in the world for the purpose of housing prisoners only and the beginning of a systematized penal system. Needless to say, it was dismal. The bridge of sighs was an enclosed walkway of stone where a prisoner got his final glance at the sky and the canals of his beloved Venice.

We then walked to San Marco or St. Mark's Basilica and Square. This was built in 830 as St. Mark's tomb. He is supposedly buried beneath the basilica. It was magnificent with a huge display of mosaics. They used only mosaics because, due to the dampness of the city on water, frescos would not be practical to last. Our guide told us that because of global warming Venice is not sinking as is thought, but the sea level is getting continuously higher.

The buildings are built on the tops of piles of logs laid sideways down to bedrock with sand and clay between. Surprisingly, it has held up for centuries. Inside of San Marco's imposing variegated marble and sculptured doorways (five in all) are precious art, rare marbles, statuary, and the mosaics beyond description. The winged lion, the symbol of St. Mark and of Venice, is everywhere.

After our tour, we had about one and a half hours of free time. So we walked everywhere we could, taking pictures of the canals, the homes, and many of the 450 ancient arched bridges throughout the city. Venice is made up of many, many little islands, and as you cross a walking bridge you enter another tiny island. Kids don't long for a car here, they beg for a motorboat, and there were some beauties. We stopped to listen to an orchestra at an outdoor restaurant and looked through the many shops and kiosks selling wonderful Venetian glass and marvelous Venetian carnival masks, which were works of art. Jack and I just looked in awe at the beauty and uniqueness around us, unable to believe that we were really here.

It was time to board our boat buses to our dock and then to the "mother" ship, and we just made it in time for dinner. We retired to our cabins early and checked our email; then Jack took a short nap to prepare for his 11:00 p.m. service for the Indonesian crew. This truly was a wonderful and exciting day. Tomorrow we tour two other islands: Murano, where there is a famous Venetian glass factory, and Burano, where exquisite lace is made. We are very much looking forward to this tour.

Monday, April 7

Today offered a glorious deep blue Venetian sky, with a light breeze to cool us. After a quick breakfast, we headed for our boat buses for our tour of Murano and Burano, islands off the shore of Venice.

It took us about a half hour to sail to Murano, a rather industrial looking island where the famous Venetian glass is created. Our boat bus docked right at the factory doors, and we were led right into what felt like the fiery furnace itself. The heat was incredible, and to imagine people working in this environment is unbelievable. We all stood on risers like a choir and watched the workers firing glass to liquid and listened to our Italian guide with excellent English and ending every single word with an "a," explain this process of glass making. Five very strong men were making a Venetian vase with a twenty-four-carat gold inlay that would sell for twenty-five thousand euros. That would be about US$37,000. It's very dangerous work to create such beauty, and it was fascinating to watch such synchronized teamwork. We watched for about fifteen minutes and then were ushered into the massive showrooms where enormous chandeliers were hung, along with mirrors of unbelievable splendor and every shape and size of glass possible. They also displayed lovely jewelry and ornaments. Jack and I managed to escape here without buying anything, much of which we could never afford. Amazing!

We boarded our boat buses again for another half-hour sail to the island of Burano. Now this was charming, with houses of many different colors lining the canals, from shocking pinks to marine blues. The legend goes that the houses are painted these colors because after an evening of much wine and revelry, the men would go into the wrong house to sleep with the wrong woman; therefore, a color coding system was necessary. Right!

We arrived at a very lovely lacemaking shop where a lacemaker was indeed making gorgeous pieces by hand. We watched in fascination as her nimble fingers whizzed along the material. We didn't get off so easily here, and I'm happy to say I bought an heirloom for our children someday. It is a beautiful red and gold Christmas tablecloth with twelve napkins in the holly pattern, all handmade and exquisite. I also bought a very lovely silk and lace blouse—oh my! We had about forty-five minutes of free time and just enjoyed walking around the little town square and taking pictures of the canals and little step bridges. It was like every picture we've ever seen of Venice and their adorable little footbridges that gently arch over each canal.

We then boarded our boats for an hour's sail back to our dock and "home" again for a late lunch. We read, checked emails, and rested during the afternoon. We and all of our table friends were together for tonight's dinner and eagerly shared our two days' experiences with each other, telling of our prize purchases. At each place tonight was a mask for us to wear for the masquerade tomorrow night. We had lots of fun taking pictures of each other in our Shrek, Mickey Mouse, Wonder Woman, etc., masks.

We came back to our cabins early tonight and went to bed, preparing for tomorrow. We sail into Split, Croatia at 5:00 a.m., and we have an 8:15 a.m. tour. We are still in the Adriatic Sea, and Croatia is an ancient city from AD 295, where the Roman emperor Diocletian built a palace on this Dalmatian coast. We understand it is another spectacular sail-in and a UNESCO World Heritage Site. We have seen quite a few UNESCO sites along our voyage. We look forward to another wonderful day tomorrow.

Tuesday, April 8

This has been quite a surprising day. It only proves you never know when you get up in the morning what is in store for you. We were up at 6:00 a.m. and after a quick breakfast went to the lounge to await our call for our tenders going ashore into Split, Croatia. Our captain came on the intercom to announce that because of hurricane winds of over 45 nautical miles per hour, our tenders could not take us to shore as planned. The swells were too high for the safety of the passengers to disembark. We were not surprised because Jack always goes out on deck while I'm getting ready, and when he came back, he said that he couldn't even get the door open as the wind was so strong.

We were all terribly disappointed but certainly appreciated the captain's decision. Especially, when later as we watched out of the library deck windows, saw the tender go out to pick up some of the new crew and musicians waiting on shore. We could hardly see the tender as it disappeared under the waves many times and several times stood straight up on end before it, thankfully, reached the ship again. We all breathed a collective sigh of relief and a "Thank you, God."

Actually, it then became a "grace" day, like when we have a snow day at home and everything is halted briefly. Jack didn't have to teach, but some other classes and activities were later scheduled. We had lunch with friends from our class and a good visit with them. Jack got caught up on his lessons, and I worked on the computer. The afternoon was devoted to exercising, reading, Sudoku, and resting. It was nice, and with tours in rapid succession, it helped to get our bearings again.

I went to a port lecture on Malta, which looks great, and I'm looking forward to docking there on Thursday. We enjoyed dinner tonight with all of us together. Our captain, as an apology for not going to Croatia, sent each table a bottle of champagne. He didn't have to apologize; we just were grateful for his caution. However, we also were sorry not only for ourselves, but for the city of Split. To have 1,800 people arrive with all the tours scheduled who were willing to spend lots of money, would have been great for their struggling economy, and Croatia could really have benefited from our being there. It was too bad, really. We came back to our cabin early tonight to get ready for a good sea day tomorrow.

Wednesday, April 9

Today was a beautiful, sunny sea day and quite a change after yesterday's fiasco in Split. Jack's interesting class was about the woman who came into the banquet in a Pharisee's home, anointed

Jesus's feet with her tears and oil, and dried them with her hair. Also dealt with why a woman, of all things, would appear at an all-male banquet in the first place. The theatre where class is held was quite full, and folks keep coming. It's wonderful. After class, I went to a port lecture on Gibraltar, our port after Malta.

We arrived at Malta by 5:00 p.m. today about twelve hours early because there was a medical emergency. One of our lady passengers had a stroke, and an ambulance was at the dock waiting for us to arrive. We have had several medical emergencies and four deaths during our voyage. Jack hasn't been called for any of the deaths but had memorial services for two guests who had loved ones die at home and one consultation with a lady whose husband died in a nursing home. Her children were there to make arrangements, and she will have a memorial service when she returns home. Life on a cruise ship is the same as at home. Considering that the average age on board is seventy-five, I'm surprised that we haven't had more deaths or emergencies. We must be a sturdy and certainly crusty lot.

After dinner we went to the show to see Hilary O'Neil, a very good comedienne and singer. The shows have been really fun with good talent. Then to bed to prepare for our tour of Valletta, Malta, tomorrow morning. Look forward to a great day tomorrow with new adventures.

Thursday, April 10

Today, we are in the port of Valletta, Malta. Our sail-in was beautiful, and golden limestone buildings of this ancient city gleamed in the warm sun. This was a strategic little island in the Mediterranean Sea and a supply route for Germany during WWII. Malta suffered much devastation. Thankfully, a lot of medieval history is still intact and magnificently restored. St. Paul was shipwrecked here on his way to Rome for trial. What a perfectly beautiful island Malta is, and our day was gloriously sunny and warm—close to 80 degrees F.

After an early breakfast, we boarded our buses, which took us to the ancient medieval town of Mdina. It is a wonderful example of a living medieval city. This was an Islamic city first built by the Romans and is incredible with its tiny narrow streets, convents, St. Paul's Co-Cathedral, and spacious squares. The doors, windows, and filigree balconies alone are stunning, and its door knockers are remarkable with animal heads and sea creatures in brass, wood, and some actually gold. Several movies, including *The Da Vinci Code*, have been filmed in Mdina. The limestone is gold colored and very much like Jerusalem. It was exactly as you would imagine a medieval city to look, and as we walked through the arched gate to look up at turrets and stone walls, we were there as far as our imaginations would take us. We had a terrific guide who made us see the St. John Knights of Malta thundering through the streets on horseback doing their gallant deeds. The beautiful St. Paul's Co-Cathedral in Mdina was built in the seventeenth century on top of a Norman church.

After Mdina, we boarded our buses for the capital city of Valletta, which is baroque in every way and a UNESCO World Heritage Site. This city—and all of Malta, really—is where gallant knights in shining armor with St. George's Cross bannered with red pointed crosses on white background became a reality. These were also called the Maltese Cross, and this was where the knights and their fair ladies once dwelled. ("Sigh!") The Grand Masters of each country's knights came together here to aid the sick and injured in the Crusades. They were the hospitalers of the ancient world and then began to offer armed escorts through hostile territories. They then became a military unit. They are the ones who built palaces, fortifications, and the St. John's Co Cathedral in Valletta. St. John's Co Cathedral is in cooperation with St. Paul's in Mdina, and Rome allowed both to exist because of their individual historic significance in Malta.

St. John's Co Cathedral was the premier cathedral of our tour. It's baroque beyond belief but because of its vast size is not gaudy and heavy looking. Each of the eight countries the knights came from had their own chapel wing with their own country's appointments, and the center nave is lined with marble slabs. Beneath each marble slab is the tomb of a knight, and each is elaborately identified by his own coat of arms. One could only become a knight from royal lineage—usually the younger sons who didn't inherit the royal estate or become priests. The Calabrian master Mattia Preti painted the ceilings, which, along with the hanging tapestries, were amazing. Caravaggio fled to Malta in the seventeenth century, and two of his masterpieces are there as well: *St. Jerome* and, perhaps his greatest work, *The Beheading of St. John.* It was overwhelming really and hard to absorb such history all at once. We definitely tried, however.

We left our wonderful guide at this point and chose to stay in Valletta to have lunch, take more pictures, and shop. The silver filigree was gorgeous, and Jack and I both purchased Maltese Crosses. We met Gary, Lona, Bob, and Jacquie along the way and enjoyed having lunch and wandering around with them. It was great fun to share this experience with such dear people as they are. By four o'clock we had to, reluctantly, walk back to the ship as we were sailing out of Malta at 5:30 p.m. We all met for dinner and marveled at our day and our good fortune for being here. Malta was a substitute for Tripoli, and I'm glad not to have missed Malta—one of our very favorite ports of call.

Hi, everyone:

This week has been a joy with so many sights to see and things to learn, both on and off ship. We're beginning to think (only think) of coming home. We still have Bermuda and New York to see and lots to do there. We are having many fun activities on ship now so people don't feel the pain of parting soon. Tonight the Osmond Brothers will be entertaining us after our formal dinner, and that'll be fun to see. Another big event will be a Concert for the Cure with our very talented cruise director, Bruce, performing. He is a graduate of Juilliard School of Music and a sterling musician. We're still working on our goal of our Race for the Cure for the Golden Anniversary of World Cruising with HAL and other events to do so. Many thousands of dollars have been raised so far and we are hopeful to raise the full fifty thousand by the end.

There will be only one more journal to send you. It's been fun for me to write, and I sincerely hope you have felt you are right here with us on this fantastic voyage.

Love to each of you and blessings to all,

Joyce and Jack

JOURNAL # 15

Friday, April 11

Today, a nice warm sea day. Glad for our warmer weather. After breakfast, I attended Jack's class, where he told of the importance of oral tradition of imparting the scriptures over the written word and reading. In the biblical world only 3 to 5 percent of the people could read and write, and the written word meant nothing to them; but because of the scribes of the day, even as arrogant as they were, we have the scriptures. Such an interesting study.

After class I attended a lecture on our port in Lisbon, Portugal. Looks wonderful and will be our last port before leaving the Mediterranean area and entering the Atlantic Ocean to begin the long voyage across to the States and home. We will briefly stop in Bermuda on the way. Today is our ninety-ninth day at sea. Amazing! We have loved every minute of it, and it does surprise us.

Worked on the computer, sent out # 14 journal installment, and then prepared for dinner and formal night. After dinner, we went to the movies and saw *Lions for Lambs* with Tom Cruise, Meryl Streep, and Robert Redford. It was a very good movie but disturbing, depressing but very thoughtful. It was a good, restful day after a wonderfully busy day in Malta yesterday. Another sea day and class tomorrow. New things to learn and people to see and enjoy.

Saturday, April 12 - 100 days at sea

It was another good sea day today. Class today was fascinating, and Jack talked about the scribes, who were a highly educated and elite group whose primary job was to reproduce the Torah. Jesus denigrates them because not only are they arrogant and seek privileges but they devour widows' estates through implying greater blessings from God by giving all they have. This therefore, makes the poor widow poorer. Great comments and questions during discussion time.

After class, I attended a lecture given by an English speaker on the Russian revolution from the time of Alexander II through Nicholas II to Stalin. It was wonderfully insightful, and I learned a lot from this dynamic speaker about Russian history I never understood before. He will give another lecture on Tuesday from Stalin to Putin and modern Russian history.

The afternoon was relaxing, and we read and rested. Tomorrow is another port day in Gibraltar. Dinner was fun with all of our table friends together. We feel so lucky to enjoy our table companions so much; as we talk with others, we learn that some are sick of their tablemates. How sad! After dinner we went to a show of a young concert pianist that was one of the funniest and best, with reminiscences of Victor Borge. A good day, and we look forward to tomorrow.

Sunday, April 13

We are now in the Strait of Gibraltar and docked at 7:00 a.m. at the Port of Gibraltar, UK. It is a beautiful sunny day, cool and comfortable for touring. We were up at 6:00 a.m., had breakfast, and then headed to our buses for our tour of "Gibraltar – City Under Siege."

We first went to the tram where we were whisked up to the top of the Rock of Gibraltar. It does indeed look just like the logo of Prudential Insurance. At the top the views of Gibraltar, Morocco, and Spain were magnificent, and the harbor is stunning. Greeting us at the top were colonies of the famous Barbary apes (really macaque monkeys). They are as cute as the dickens and are scampering everywhere. They are little thieves, and we had to not carry anything in a plastic bag because they identify plastic bags with food. They grab it, and you lose whatever it holds. We were warned not to feed or touch them, as they bite. However, they love to jump on someone's shoulders or head and certainly surprised many of us with that treat. It was fun to see them, and they are little hams and actually pose for pictures.

Gibraltar is on the tip of the Iberian Peninsula and has historically been an important military base for the British. Right now Spain wants it back from the British, but the population prefers to be with England instead. It will be interesting to see how this comes out. However, whoever has Gibraltar maintains control of access to the Mediterranean Sea. An important holding, to be sure.

We then went to the Great Siege Tunnels dug into the huge rock, and this small country has been under fourteen sieges because it is so strategic. These were ingenious defensive caves, really, with cannons and artillery, etc. Walking through the tunnels, which were dark, wet, close, and steep, was difficult. These tunnels were essential to the Allied efforts in WWII. We then went to Europa Point, its southernmost point, to see the Pillars of Hercules: the Rock of Gibraltar in Europe and Mount Abyla in Morocco. The legend is that at one time Africa and Europe were joined at this juncture, as they are only seventeen miles apart, and Hercules brought his ax down between them to make the water in the Atlantic drain into and create the Mediterranean Sea. Historically, it was an earthquake but, oh well! It was exciting to see two continents—Africa and Europe—and three countries—Gibraltar, Spain, and Morocco—from this point.

As we drove to the Gibraltar Museum, we passed the enormous Moorish Castle complex and Moorish Baths built in AD 742;

incredible and beautifully preserved. At the museum, we learned that the first human skull discovered was in Gibraltar and it was ignored for forty years until a similar skull was discovered in Germany, and that was identified as the German Neanderthal Man. If Gibraltar had identified theirs first, it would have been Gibraltar Woman instead of Neanderthal. This is interesting, indeed. The Battle of Trafalgar was fought here, and Nelson's body was brought to Gibraltar on its route to England preserved in a barrel of brandy. He was surely pickled and now is buried at St. Paul's Cathedral in London next to the architect Christopher Wren.

We drove back to the ship in time for lunch and were able to have a nap before dinner. At 3:00 p.m. we had a giant ship's garage sale on the Lido Deck for clothing and/or souvenirs that people bought and then had second thoughts when they brought it to the ship. We're starting to think about packing up now, and how do we get all this stuff home? It was hilarious what people sold and what people bought. All the proceeds go to the Susan G. Komen Fund for Breast Cancer. We raised over $600 in nickels and dimes. It was great fun.

After dinner, went to the show of jugglers and a singer and comedienne which was a very good variety show. Jack is off to his 11:00 p.m. service for the crew. Our passenger service was at 5:00 p.m. with a really good attendance. Tomorrow we dock at Lisbon, Portugal, and we have a seven-and-a-half-hour tour. This is one port I am really anxious to see.

Monday, April 14

Today at 8:00 a.m. we docked at the Lisbon Harbor. What a beautiful sail-in and city, with its red tiled roofs and pretty architecture. There are blue and white tiles of lovely designs on even the modern buildings downtown. Even the street signs on buildings show these lovely blue and white tiles. We ate a hardy breakfast because this is a long (seven and a half hour) tour day. We boarded our buses to meet our guide, who was a wealth of interesting information and spoke perfect English. We drove along the coast of the Tagus River from the Lisbon Harbor until we reached the lighthouse and the farthest point west in Europe pointing to the US. Then at the mouth of Tagus River began the Atlantic Ocean. We drove through lovely countryside, quite mountainous, to the seaside town of Cascais, a beautiful little town with white beaches, popular with Portuguese young people. The little streets were just wide enough for two people to pass and had wonderful window boxes overhead filled with flowers. There were cute shops and bakeries along the way filled with items of Portuguese handicraft and goodies and, of course, the black rooster on everything, the symbol of Portuguese good luck. The area is charming and very pedestrian friendly with cobblestones in variegated colors everywhere; just lovely. Our weather was perfect for wandering along the coast—in the 60s and sunny all the way.

An hour later, we boarded our buses for the forty-five-minute journey to the fairy tale mountain town of Sintra. The poet Lord Byron described the beauty of Sintra's mountain ranges in his poem, *Childe Harold*. This is one of Portugal's oldest villages and contains the royal family's summer residence, the fourteenth-century Pena Palace. Lovely, with the filigree windows and tiles over the exterior. At the very top of the mountain over the center of town was the huge Moorish Castle and fortification. Rome ruled from 205 BC until the Moors (Muslims) captured Portugal in the eighth century. Then in AD 1147, Crusaders recaptured it for the Christians. Seeing all of these magnificent countries and learning the history on site helps us understand our Christian heritage and the role of the Crusades in a whole new way.

We saw large areas of Cork Oak trees; cork has been an economic staple of Portugal in the past centuries. That no longer is the case. In our shopping forays in Sintra the gorgeous tiles lined with cork were fun items to bring home. The embroidery work and lace are also exquisite. We were taken to a lovely restaurant in Sintra's town square for a delicious Portuguese lunch. The wine and bread as well as luscious desserts were outstanding. Full and sleepy after that huge meal, we boarded for the hour's ride back to Lisbon. Jack and I vowed to return to Sintra one day. Of course, we've said that at several of our stops. Even a week wouldn't be enough of this wonderfully quaint area of Europe. It is also one of the few places left in the world that is still reasonably affordable.

We drove back along the Atlantic coast, stopping at the Tower of Belem (meaning Bethlehem). It looks like an enormous chess piece and is the symbol of Portuguese national heritage. The tower was built on the Tagus River with a structure of Our Lady of Safe Homecoming on top to welcome seafarers home. Across the Tagus is the 752 foot figure representing Christ the Redeemer with outstretched arms, looking very like the same-named statue in Lisbon's sister city, Rio de Janeiro. They have very strong ties with Brazil. We also stopped for photos of the Monument of Discoveries, a beautiful tribute to Portugal's supremacy in navigation and those brave people.

We then drove back to our ship, passing long, beautifully arched aqueducts. These are not Roman but were built in 1748 AD for their water source in the mountains. We got to our ship in time to prepare for dinner and our beautiful sail away from Lisbon Harbor. We are also sailing away from Mainland Europe into the Atlantic. Our next stop, but still in Europe, is Madeira, Portugal. We arrive there on Wednesday.

After a long, tiring, and busy day, we came back to our cabin after dinner. Sent out emails and then to bed. We are hoping for a good, restful sea day tomorrow. That's what is so wonderful about cruising: when you feel you just cannot go another step, a very welcome, restful sea day is given. It was a truly beautiful day today.

Tuesday, April 15

Today is cloudy, and we're sailing west, leaving Europe's mainland toward Funchal, Madeira, Portugal. People tell us this is a beautiful island to explore, and we're looking forward to it. Class was great today, and Jack told about the parable of the unjust steward. A fascinating study. It was hard to stop discussing when we had to leave the theatre at 10:00 a.m. Jack and I then had to go to the cruise director's office for a video shoot of all of us clergy and spouses waving for the farewell video being prepared for the passengers as they leave in just twelve days. Sigh! I'm in complete denial.

I went to another lecture this a.m. about modern Russia from Stalin to Putin. It was so helpful in understanding why and how Russia has the leadership it now has. The only single difference today from the Czarist time is that Putin by Constitution must leave the presidency, and no one knows what the new president really will do. Russia has had a long, long history of utter bedlam and economic tragedy.

After lunch we attempted to see the personnel from HAL about shipping some of our luggage home. There were too many ahead of us, so we decided not to wait, but we bought a large carton and will see the representative another day. We hope to take as little luggage as possible with us by plane. We rested this afternoon, Jack put our photos into the computer, and I worked on the journal for sending on Friday.

We all met for dinner tonight and had such a fun time together. Came back to our cabin early to prepare for tomorrow's tour in Madeira. It was a good day.

Wednesday, April 16

Today we are in the beautiful island of Madeira, Portugal, one of Europe's prettiest ports. Flowers are blooming everywhere, and this is the native home of the flower, Bird of Paradise, which is grown and exported throughout the world. Of course, also grapes thrive here on "perfect" volcanic soil that is nutrient rich; the result is Madeira wines. We docked after a beautiful sail-in at 8:00 a.m., and after breakfast we headed out to our buses for a long day touring this island, Winston Churchill's favorite vacation spot. Again, lovely yellow and white stucco buildings with red tiled roofs. Our weather quickly became too warm for our jackets so we could happily leave them on our buses.

Our first stop was the little town of Brava with cobblestone streets and sidewalks of variegated colors and designs. We toured the gorgeous and spectacular countryside of western Madeira. We drove past lush, terraced farms and gardens in steep mountainous terrain. Terracing is the only way they can farm, and they produce an amazing abundance of crops from such a small island. Grape arbors and banana and sugar cane plantations cover this island. We, of course, drove up the highest mountain ever on this tour and arrived well above the timberline. The view of the Atlantic coastline and the whole island was incredible, and we have never been so high except in a plane. It took about an hour of continuous hairpin curves in a bus the size of Vermont to get there. This was some powerful machine to get us up, and from there the farmlands looked like a very small patchwork quilt. What a treat we received with clouds and sun mingling in these fabulous peaks and valleys. Our photos can't touch the glory of it all, and we felt like birds that high—over 2,000 feet.

As we drove down, we saw many waterfalls and flowers along the way. The capital city's name, Funchal, means the herb "fennel" because it covered the island when the Portuguese came in the fifteenth century. We went through other lovely villages such as Porto Moniz and stopped in São Vicente to walk around its narrow streets and visit a lovely cemetery. We were then taken to lunch at a Madeira restaurant on the precipice of a mountain that juts out over the ocean. Here we could look down under walkways to natural seawater pools in the jagged peaks. Guests also could swim in the pools. We had a delicious lunch of the local black fish—very ugly, with huge teeth—which was delicious with a white flesh and mild flavor. Again, the white and red Madeira wines flowed like water and were probably safer. It's amazing that people can even walk here after drinking so much wine at all meals. After lunch the shopping was great, especially with the handmade knits and embroidery everywhere. I bought a lovely hand knit sweater for only 28 euros (US$32).

After lunch and a long winding drive down and across the mountain range and through many, many tunnels (there are over a hundred of them), we stopped at a beautiful beach resort on the coast where we strolled and rested along the beach. Had a little rain while in the upper mountains, but the beach area was warm and sunny, and people were swimming in the Atlantic surf. We then came into the capital, Funchal, and headed back to the ship. Madeira was the home of Christopher Columbus, and the legend goes that as he was sitting on the shore gazing out to sea, he discovered driftwood on the shore that had come from far-off lands, and this was the inspiration of his navigational dreams and ultimately his discoveries.

We came back to the ship in time for a short rest and dinner. Only Lona and Gary were able to meet for dinner with us tonight. Since the guys were beat after our day in Madeira, Lona and I went to the movie, a cute "chick flick"—a girls' night out. It was fun. Then to bed and another welcome sea day tomorrow.

At 6:00 p.m., while having dinner, we sailed away from the last of Europe and will be sailing transatlantic toward Bermuda for five whole days. We can feel a rougher sea now, and soon no land will be in sight. We are now all beginning to feel the "pull" of home. Only ten days left of this remarkable journey.

It's a bouncy sea day today but sunny and pleasant. Quite rough this evening, and we needed to hold onto railings while walking.

Jack's interesting class considered "No one can serve two masters" (Matthew 6:24 NRSV). Comments and questions were great. After class we met with our shipping company and discovered we could ship a huge cardboard box with no weight limits for only $75.00. That will take care of all our excess easily. Thank heavens.

Then Jack and I went to the Midday Madness sale on Lido Deck, where everything was priced at $10. I replaced my Timex watch, which gave up at the start of the voyage, and a pair of sunglasses. Jack found a nice leather nail kit. People were buying things like they were giving them away—amazing! The stuff was of good quality.

After lunch I just slept for two hours. I was catching up, I guess. We read, Jack downloaded our pictures into the computer, and then we went to dinner. We were all there except Bob and Jacquie, who were greatly missed. Back to our cabin after dinner for an early night. We sure needed the rest. We look forward to a good sea day tomorrow. We set our clocks back another hour tonight, which helps us catch up on our rest. We are now only 3 hours different from NY and tonight we turn back our clocks again. This is how we gain back the day we lost going over the International Date Line. It is one hour at a time. We are meeting ourselves going.

Hi, everyone:

I cannot believe this is my last installment. It has been a fantastic adventure, and my last day's entry says it all. Thank you all for being such faithful readers, and I have dearly loved your comments and good wishes along the way. May God bless each of you in your days to come.

My love and good wishes to each of you,
Lovingly,

Joyce

JOURNAL # 16

Friday, April 18

It's another bouncy sea day in the Atlantic. No other ship or land in sight for two days. Seems strange after being in the Mediterranean for so long in such a busy trade route. In Jack's class we are beginning a three-part series on the Good Samaritan. These parables are full of little gems you never see until you know first-century culture. Amazing!

After class I attended Barbara's port lecture on Bermuda. It sounds beautiful. I then attended another lecture on conscientiousness from a motivational speaker, the sort that conventions and corporations hire. It was interesting but very "me"-centered. Quite a contrast after Jack's "God-centered" class. However, there were many good points. I came away from the "me"-centered lecture with the feeling of not having quite grown up. It wasn't enough. There's got to be more, and I realized that only with a God-centered and faith-based life can there ever be more. That's when you can reach out from yourself to others. That is when it becomes "More."

We had a quiet lunch with Lona and Gary and a restful afternoon reading and working on the computer. Jean and Dick invited all of us table friends to tea at their cabin. It was lovely and we so enjoy these dear people.

It was formal night tonight with a delicious dinner and the

string quartet playing above us. After dinner came a really good entertainment: the Osmond Brothers sang and danced and entertained us royally. You can certainly tell why they are famous and others are not. They are not only talented but galaxies above others in their stage presence and performance. They are good, and we hated for the show to end.

We came back to our cabin for bed and were able to send out our # 15 journal installment. Only one more to send next week. We turn our clocks back another hour tonight and another good sea day tomorrow.

Saturday, April 19 – Passover

What a wonderful sea day today. Jack's class was so engaging as he continued in the second of the series on the Good Samaritan. He explained the rules and restrictions on priests and Levites for purity and what was really involved in their *not* being involved. Fascinating! After class Bob and Jacquie invited us to their cabin to see their pictures, which they are preparing for a bound coffee table book of the Grand Voyage. The photography is absolutely professional quality, and it will be a magnificent tribute to our trip.

I checked our email and had the internet manager assist me in a problem. I didn't know how to eliminate "cookies"—not the yummy eating kind, but the internet kind. I was having difficulty paying some bills online because of too many "cookies." Yikes! We had lunch and then rested and read, and I did Sudoku the afternoon away.

We then had a most wonderful invitation to the Jewish seder at dinnertime. HAL provided a beautiful Passover celebration for all of us, and Rabbi Bob and Sheila invited everyone who wanted to come. Some 240 people attended, and Rabbi Bob officiated the seder. Bob and Sheila had Father Bill and us sit with them, and it was an honor to do so. They told a great story of our chief wine steward who at port after port was unable to find a Passover sweet wine necessary for the celebration. When we were touring in Gibraltar, Bob and Sheila just happened to pass a Jewish deli that also sold kosher Passover wine. Sheila asked the proprietor if he had cases of this wine. He said yes, he did, so Sheila was able to get hold of the chief steward, and he went to the shop and bought many, many cases of it for the ship. Now that was one lucky and very happy deli owner, believe me. It was a sweet kosher wine that was indeed delicious. We had a wonderful celebration with our Jewish friends, several of whom attend Jack's class daily. In fact, many of our Christian class members were there. The songs were fun to sing, and the saxophone player in our orchestra is Jewish and played the beautiful haunting songs as we came in and sang. It was really a terrific evening.

After the seder dinner Jack went to the movies for a film he wanted to see, and I came back to the cabin to read. It was a great sea day, and I saw my first whale off the starboard side while having coffee in the Lido. *Wow!* Just saw one whale, and it was huge. What a thrill it was, and now I'm a certified seaman or seawoman.

Sunday, April 20 – only one week left

It was another sea day. Worship was at 9:00 a.m. today. In Jack's sermon he spoke of gratitude and if "why me?" for difficulties, then "why me?" for good things and privileges as well. This was our last worship service, and many people said their goodbyes— some tearfully, as several people will be disembarking in New York City on Thursday. The sadness felt like our leaving another church family. We have become very close in our four months together and have made many good friends.

After class Jack and I went to Barbara's port lecture on New York City. We look forward to that beautiful port and hope to see the choristers in the Medieval Museum of the Metropolitan

Museum in NYC. It was Barbara's last lecture, and we gave her a rousing standing ovation. She has been the best port lecturer we've ever had on cruises. She was very touched.

I then went to a lecture on handwriting analysis. It was fun, and I learned how different personality traits can be determined just by the way one writes the letter *t*. It was so very interesting. After lunch we went to a "Concert for the Cure" performed on piano by Bruce, our very talented cruise director. It was very good, and the Queen's Lounge was packed. We bought tickets, and all proceeds went to the Susan G. Komen Foundation. There will be another walk this week—our final event—and hopefully we'll reach our "golden" goal for our golden anniversary voyage.

Gary and Lona treated all of us table friends at the special Pinnacle Grill tonight for dinner. It was lovely, and dear Bob and Jacquie presented each couple with 8 x 10 pictures of ourselves during different activities and tours. They were wonderful and so professionally done. They also had a bag of goodies for each of us, with thoughtfully selected fun gifts and notes commemorating our tours and ports and our times together. Each note and little goody was perfectly suited to each of us. Such caring and thoughtful spirits they are.

We came back to our cabin to prepare for tomorrow's sea day and alas, to think about packing. Jack is off to his last worship service for the crew. He said it will be hard to say goodbye to these dear young men who are a definite minority on the ship because of their Christianity. They do have a difficult time in the Muslim world in which they live and work. Jack asks for prayers for these young men for strength in their faith.

Monday, April 21

Rocky sea day today with temps in the high 60s—nice. We're on our way to Bermuda and anchor in Hamilton at 8:00 a.m. About

750 of our passengers will be tendered into shore by Hamilton ferries all at once. Must be a huge ferryboat. We have been in some of the most unusual ferries and boats around the world, as our ship is too large to dock at some of the piers.

Jack completed his three-part series on the Good Samaritan today. He told of the bitter hatred the Jews had for the Samaritans and what a risk the Samaritan took, risking his very life to aid the man robbed and left for dead. Several of our class members said goodbye, as they will leave us in New York City on Thursday. There is only one more class left before we all disembark in Florida.

We spent most of the day calling to have our cable connected at home in Easton and other necessities. We wrote many letters of thank-you and appreciation to many people. We then prepared for our last formal dinner tonight. It was the Black and Gold Ball and banquet, and our dining room was decorated with enormous black and gold balls, streamers, stars, and star balloons everywhere. It was stunning, with all the men in their black tuxes and the ladies dressed in gold and black gowns. I have never seen such gold jewelry and every gold glittering thing imaginable. It was quite beautiful and very elegant to behold.

After dinner we went to a wonderful show of a British singer, Iris Williams, who had a voice that sounded much like Edith Piaf, the French singer in the early twentieth century. She entertained us beautifully for an hour with lovely melodies. Then it was back to our cabin to prepare for tomorrow's tour in Bermuda. We are really looking forward to being there, and after five days of rather rough seas, land will seem nice. It will be an early day tomorrow.

Tuesday, April 22

We must be a crusty lot because after five days of rough seas, there were no barf bags at the elevators, and the dining room has been quite full. It was very unlike when we first began the cruise. It was a gorgeous, sunny, warm day in the high 60s as we anchored off Hamilton harbor early today. The harbor was beautiful and the large capital city of Hamilton had very pretty architecture with rather square, simple lines of structure. Pastel colors of pink, blue, purple, green and cream were on the stucco exterior, with the most unusual concrete roofs, which were whitewashed with lime and bleach to purify the rain water as it is collected into each house or building's cistern beneath. It's a very efficient system actually. The beaches are beautiful, with pink sand. Bermuda is a coral island with huge coral reefs around it. In fact, Bermuda comprises several islands.

After breakfast we boarded our monstrous 750-passenger ferry for tendering to shore. It was not pleasant, with such a crush of people boarding at once. When we disembarked, we boarded cute little pink and blue buses for our tour, Highlights of Hamilton and St. George's Island. We first headed, guess what, to the highest peak on the island which was only two hundred meters above the harbor. Nothing compared to other ports of 2,000 feet. We drove through lush, beautiful countryside and saw areas of rich farmland and groves. The view from our first stop at St. David's Lighthouse was spectacular. The water is vividly blue, in various shades because of the coral reefs, which are a darker blue. The sky also could not have been bluer or the white clouds fluffier. Our guide called it a perfect Bermuda day. He thanked us for bringing such good weather as it had rained for two weeks straight. Lucky us!

We then drove to the island of St. George—a pretty little harbor town with quaint shops and cafés all over—and then to lovely St. Peter's Church, the island's oldest. We strolled around looking in shops and visiting with the people and our ship friends. We were then able to go back to Hamilton along the beautiful coastline and stopped at the Verdmont house museum. This was a magnificent Georgian-style home built in 1710 by of all things, a pirate, called a "privateer." He basically pirated Spanish ships carrying silver and gold. This man was so rich he makes Donald Trump look a beggar. It was a wonderful home that has been owned by only two families, and everything remains original and unchanged down through the centuries.

It was time to go back to the ferry and to our ship. We got back with little time to prepare for dinner. We went to the Amsterdam Singers and Dancers show, which was terrific. The costumes were gorgeous.

When Jack had his last crew worship on Sunday, they gave him a beautiful batik shirt they purchased for him in Bali, where most of the crew live, and they gave me a lovely tapestry bag from Venice. I love it, and it will always remind me of those dear, dear men who are such wonderful people. Jack wore his shirt the next day to meals and class, and all the crew recognized immediately that it was from Bali, and their beautiful smiles said it all. They have so appreciated Jack's ministry to them as well as our passengers. It was a wonderful bonus for both of us to be so welcomed by the crew, a bonus that we didn't expect. It was a beautiful day in Bermuda; we loved being there and want to come again.

Wednesday, April 23

A sea day today and a very, very busy one. There was no class because of our disembarkation program in the Queen's Lounge at 10:30 a.m. It's always a touching program of the staff and crew saying their goodbyes. Our clergy video of waving goodbye was played, with each department waving as well.

Had lunch with Bob and Jacquie to make plans for tomorrow's time in NYC. After lunch we began packing up as much as we could in our large carton for shipping and making lists of our purchases and where they were from for our customs declaration in Fort Lauderdale. I'm not surprised that we'll have to pay about $200 for our overage allowance. What were we thinking? Oh, but what fun it was. We sent emails and made calls. Then we prepared for dinner—our last time with Dick and Jean because they leave us in NYC tomorrow.

It was a good time at dinner tonight, and we decided that since none of us have had a birthday or anniversary celebration in our four months together, we would have a non-birthday party. So we ordered a birthday cake from culinary, and all the waiters and wine stewards sang "Happy Birthday" to us in their language. It was wonderful, and we love them all. It was a tearful goodbye for us and Dick and Jean, so the rest of us planned to send an email to them tonight to welcome them back home in New Jersey.

We came back to our cabin early and to bed. An early day tomorrow as we sail into NYC. I have never seen the Statue of Liberty by boat, and we'll take the Circle Cruise tour out of the NY harbor over to Ellis Island and the Statue. We are really looking forward to a great day tomorrow. Our last tour of our journey. Can't believe it.

Thursday, April 24

Wow! We are home, and Jack took lots of pictures as we sailed past the Statue of Liberty and into NYC Harbor. What a beautiful sail-in it was. We had breakfast and waited for immigration to call us alphabetically to go ashore. We had to wait for all those leaving us in NYC, and then the ship's tours had to go after. As we were waiting for our turn to go ashore, Bruce, our cruise director, told everyone to go out the back deck for a wonderful surprise, and we saw a plane go by about 10 times flying a huge banner "Welcome Home, MS *Amsterdam* World Voyagers." There wasn't a dry eye on deck.

Bob and Jacquie and we were on our own today to just cruise the harbor and walk around the city. We finally were able to leave the ship and walked three blocks to the Circle Cruise Line for the tour by boat. Somehow a bus tour didn't seem appropriate in NYC. I was not prepared for the emotion of being on home soil and greeting our own people. I realized that we are as friendly with open smiles as anyone around the world—even in NYC. We couldn't help smiling at everyone we met, and they smiled back, even the little children on school trips.

New York from the Hudson River is really beautiful. We each shared our feelings about our voyage, and we all felt that after having seen the Taj Mahal, the pyramids, the Suez Canal, and Istanbul, now NYC is the perfect finale of it all. We are *so* fortunate to be American with our warts and all. It also surprises us (and it shouldn't) that when people hear what we have done, they are in awe and amazement, and on our tour the boat guide said, "In pier 92 is the MS *Amsterdam* just arrived after a 114-day around-the-world cruise." It then hit each of us just how blessed and privileged we have been to have this incredible experience.

Another terrific thing today: after our tour seeing the Statue of Liberty, Ellis Island, the Empire State Building, and Ground Zero from the water, we had a great lunch at a pretty little café, outdoors in 80 degrees weather in NYC in springtime. We each ordered a cheeseburger, fries, and a Coke. It was heavenly and so American. Forget the cholesterol. We're home!

We came back to the ship, still our home until Sunday, and rested an hour before our sail away with the band playing "Anchors Away" and flags flying out of NY Harbor on our way to Fort Lauderdale, our starting point. We then went to dinner and met a new couple at our table from Canada who joined our ship and will continue on to Vancouver through the Panama Canal. We all wished we were going with them.

We came back to our cabin, and Jack is getting ready for his last class tomorrow morning. It will be painful to say goodbye to this church family. It will be a good sea day tomorrow as we sail along our own eastern coastline.

A beautiful, warm sea day as we sail south. Jack saw about a hundred dolphins in our wake this morning, and our table friends saw several whales on their way migrating north. Busy time of year for sea life.

Jack's class was quite full, even though about ten left us in NYC. By request he talked farther about the development of life after death in the scriptures. Some had missed his last lecture earlier about it. This was a day of many "lasts," and our last class was a tearful and painful one for all of us as we said our goodbyes and everyone expressed their appreciation to Jack. He was very touched by their appreciation and good wishes to both of us. We had lunch with Jack and Lorraine, a wonderful Jewish couple who have enjoyed our class and said they learned so much about their own faith background. We spent the afternoon doing domestic things and getting our possessions organized.

This evening we attended the Jewish Sabbath, and it was beautiful. We, of course, didn't understand the Hebrew, but it was easy to sense the worshipfulness of it, and we were able to pray our prayers of thanksgiving with the congregation. We will miss Bob and Sheila and promise to keep in touch with the hope we will be on another cruise together in the future. We went to dinner with our table friends and so enjoyed our time with them trading stories and tips for customs and packing as we each learn what to do in the disembarking process. I have a feeling it'll be a zoo because we have to go to customs officials at 6:00 a.m. privately if we exceed our customs limit, and we certainly have.

After dinner several of us staff members (funny people) agreed to meet in the Crow's Nest for a little party for our last time together. It was so good to have met these wonderful and dedicated people. We will miss them as well.

To cheer ourselves up, we went to the show tonight and saw a beautiful and talented opera singer, Dorothy Bishop. Not only was she immensely talented, but she was lots of fun too. To bed now and getting ready for a busy day, seriously packing up tomorrow. After four months we've become very possessive of our little space, and it feels like we're moving from a family home and community, as we actually are. It'll be a good day tomorrow—our last sea day.

Saturday, April 26

Well, here we are, our last day on ship. It has been 113 and a half days, and we will have sailed 36,000 miles around the world. Unbelievable! We will be back in Fort Lauderdale tonight at 9:00 p.m., and guess what? The world really is round.

Had a leisurely breakfast with dear friends Jacquie and Bob, and then checked emails and sent some thank-you notes to some of our class members who have wished us well. Then we had lunch with Sharon and Ron, our ballroom dancing instructors, who are very interesting and fun people from Canada. Back to our cabin to pack, and we have done it. Everything went into our bags with absolutely nothing to spare. We put the proper tags on everything, and the bags go into the hallway at 9:00 p.m. tonight.

We will be having our final dinner soon with our table friends. It will be painful, but all have signed up for the 2010 World Cruise, and we're all praying that we will get that assignment too. All that's left now is a good dinner and early to bed as we meet with customs early tomorrow. Then we will be on our way home to Easton. Can't believe it's over so soon. It was the fastest four months of our lives.

This was the Golden Voyage of Holland America Line, and there were many, many treasures we have had and with Barbara's help I want to list all the gold we have seen and experienced:

- Golden beans of coffee in Vietnam
- Golden tree frogs in Polynesia

- Golden horn in Istanbul
- Golden wine at dinner
- Golden sunrises many, many days
- Golden sunsets just as many
- Golden fleece in Greece
- Golden beaches in Malta
- Golden jewelry everywhere
- Golden Buddha in Singapore
- Golden fish in Hong Kong
- Golden altar at St. Marks in Venice
- Golden caviar in Russia
- Golden friends forever
- Golden memories that will always be ours

Jack and I have been blessed beyond our wildest dreams. This gift has changed us as human beings relating to other human beings around this magnificent world of ours. We have learned that we love it beyond measure, and we so need to care for it as the precious treasure that it is. In our retirement we feel we may have had our day in the sun. But the sunset can be still bright, warm, and dazzling.

Thank you, God.

Joyce

CPSIA information can be obtained
at www.ICGtesting.com
Printed in the USA
LVHW090308260421
685571LV00004B/52